So You Have to Write an Economics Term Paper...

Lawrence H. Officer
Daniel H. Saks
Judith A. Saks

Illustrations by
Patricia M. Mullaly

1981
Michigan State University Press
East Lansing

ISBN: 0-87013-229-6

Library of Congress Catalog Card Number: 80-80313

Copyright © 1980
By the Board of Trustees of Michigan State University
East Lansing, Michigan. All rights reserved

Printed in the United States of America

This book is dedicated
to our late colleague and friend
HERBERT KISCH

who sparked an interest in
scholarship and writing
among generations of undergraduates
at Michigan State University

Contents

Introduction   ix

Part I
How to Write an Economics Term Paper

1. A Term Paper — And It's Too Late To Drop
The Course
An overview of the problem   3

2. What Can I Tell The Prof Who
Knows It All Anyway?
*The scope for originality; what is a
contribution; performing well at your
own level; everyone's an expert in something*   6

3. Picking A Question That Wouldn't Strain The
Resources Of The Ford Foundation To Answer!
How to find a topic   9

4. Now That I've Got The Question,
How Do I Get An Answer?
*Choosing a strategy; accident
favors the prepared mind; being flexible*   14

5. You Have To Open Your Mouth Before
You Can Brush Your Teeth
*Breaking down the problem into small,
sequential tasks with intermediate deadlines*   17

6. You Can't Tell It Like It Is If
You Don't Understand It
Analysis, description, opinion, and emotion   20

7. Facts, True Facts, And False Facts
Types of evidence   24

8. Finding Out What's Known Even When It's Wrong
   How to do library research, including
   books, journals, documents, and newspapers   30

9. It's OK To Talk To Strangers
   How to conduct an interview or take a survey   39

10. Numbers Are Real And Imaginary
    How to use statistics   46

11. If It's Straight From The Horse's Mouth,
    You Had Better Name The Horse
    Avoiding plagiarism,
    preparing footnotes and bibliographies   52

12. Getting It Together And Cutting And Pasting
    The writing itself, and the
    importance of editing and revising   60

Part II

The Best Papers from the *M.S.U. Economist*

Log Export Restrictions
   Richard Craswell   69

The Economic Effects of Billboard Control
   Brant Freer and Ronald Sutton   81

Medicaid and the Emergency Room
   John S. MacDonald   93

An Analysis of the Demand for Illicit Marijuana in a
University Community and Projecting for the Results
of a Tax on Legalized Marijuana
   Christopher Mallin   106

Poverty and the Distribution of Income and Wealth
in Eighteenth-Century Suffolk County
   John B. Palmer   115

A Study of the Relationship between External
Diseconomies and Population
    Christine Schneider Schafer and Daniel Watson   129

The Increased Price to Students of Living Closer
to the University
                             Craig Weaver   138

Introduction

For nine years, the Department of Economics, Michigan State University, has published an annual journal of undergraduate papers, the *M.S.U. Economist*. We initiated the project because we thought analytic writing skills were important and because the Department of English was not prepared to undertake the task of teaching our students expository writing. We believed publication would not only reward those who wrote well but also provide a model of outstanding research papers. We were surprised at how interesting many of the papers were. The *M.S.U. Economist* has actually been a lively journal (faint praise, perhaps, by our professional standards), and undergraduates have generally been enthusiastic about it.

We are pleased to see what we hope is a trend toward more emphasis on the skills represented by these types of papers. Recently, Harvard followed in MSU's footsteps by publishing a similar undergraduate journal, appropriately entitled the *Harvard College Economist*. Business and government, in their recruitment and promotion efforts, are placing increasing emphasis on clear exposition and analysis. And spurred by the collapsing market for English Ph.D.'s, we may even see more teaching of expository writing to undergraduates.

This book is meant to celebrate the continued publication of the *M.S.U. Economist* through a period when rising class sizes made the assignment of undergraduate research papers an almost Herculean task. It is also meant to share more widely the experiences we have had with assigning and editing such papers. We are happy to report to those who may have despaired that undergraduate writing in economics is alive and well at Michigan State University, and no doubt elsewhere.

The talented undergraduates who have contributed to the *M.S.U. Economist* are represented by the seven outstanding papers (two jointly authored) included here as the best in the first eight years of the journal's existence. The authors and the years in which their contributions appeared are as follows: Christopher Mallin, 1971; John S. MacDonald, 1972; Richard Craswell, 1973; John B. Palmer, 1973; Christine Schneider Schafer and Daniel Watson, 1973; Craig Weaver, 1975; and Brant Freer and Ronald Sutton, 1976.

Several people worked behind the scenes to produce this volume. Dole A. Anderson provided needed interest, encouragement, and advice. Linda Dewit generously shared her bibliographical knowledge. Elizabeth Johnston's contribution went beyond that of production editor to include substantive suggestions for improving the volume. Jean Moeller was instrumental in locating authors of the student papers and in arranging for publication of the *M.S.U. Economist* over the years. To these individuals our sincere appreciation.

Part I

How to Write an Economics Term Paper

A TERM PAPER-AND IT'S TOO LATE TO DROP THE COURSE

COURSE REQUIREMENTS

COURSE REQUIREMENTS

CHAPTER 1

An overview of the problem

Scientists have failed to identify a special gene for the ability to write good term papers. It is an acquired skill, although some seem to master it more easily than others. The very fact that you are reading this book means that you recognize you may have a problem. What you may not realize is that it is one widely shared and, as are many problems, solvable only with concerted effort.

3

You can become a good writer, and if you do, you will have a strong competitive edge in our society. A college education is no longer a rarity, but someone who can write a correct, lucid, concise, and interesting analysis of a problem is of special value in almost any occupation. Consider the plant supervisor who wants higher management to undertake a new investment program, the sales manager who wants to devise a new marketing plan, the teacher who wants to institute a new curriculum, the government worker who needs to evaluate a new program, the scientist who wants to try a new line of research. They all need to be able to define the problem, identify and evaluate various solutions, and convince decision makers and workers to implement their ideas. Learning to write a good term paper is one way of acquiring and practicing these skills.

This book is our attempt to help you learn to write good term papers in economics and business courses. The best way we know to do that is by example, and that is the unique feature of this book. We have included seven of the best papers published in the *M.S.U. Economist,* an annual journal of undergraduate economics papers we have helped edit for the past nine years. Better than anything we might write, they demonstrate the range of undergraduate creativity and the potential for sound economic analysis at the undergraduate level.

We have also included, in the first part of this book, some advice undergraduates have found helpful. We understand that writing an analytical research paper can be an unsettling experience. Everyone has his or her own style of accomplishing it. We want to concentrate on the basics and will emphasize a few points. First, you should have confidence in your ability to say something important. Second, you need to pick a narrow and well-defined topic or problem so your task will be manageable. Third, you need to break the problem down into small, sequential tasks for which you establish intermediate deadlines; this is so the project does not suddenly overwhelm you toward the end of the term when you have plenty of other work to do. Fourth, you need to outline a relevant and effective research strategy using the resources available to you. Fifth, you need to communicate your findings clearly, without unnecessary rambling.

In short, writing a term paper is not one but several activities requiring different skills and considerable management. We can offer some guidance based on our experience in advising hundreds of undergraduates over the past nine years; we can provide examples; we can suggest some other books on the subject. But, frankly, we do not know how to teach you to write a term paper. We know that all sorts of students who thought they could not write a paper were amazed to discover that serious analysis of an interesting topic can be exciting and can draw out of them resources that they never suspected they had. Some of the most creative papers we have seen were done by students who did poorly on multiple-choice exams and had come to doubt their own capacities.

CHAPTER 2

The scope for originality; what is a contribution; performing well at your own level; everyone's an expert in something

What every student always finds hard to believe is that he or she is an expert in something. You know a lot about the town where you grew up, your neighborhood, your dormitory, your summer jobs, your parents' jobs, your school, and many other topics. Because you are or were an insider somewhere at some time, you are in a special position to understand how some particular economic institution works. You can talk to fellow workers, neighbors, supervisors, and all sorts of other people who are likely to be candid and helpful. Of course, there is a problem. It is difficult to be objective about situations in which you are personally involved, so it often helps to pick a topic which makes use of your experience in some indirect way. But the point is that you do have experience.

Let us illustrate with some examples. A student who has searched for off-campus living quarters realizes, when he studies rent gradients in an urban economics course, that he can test the theory against his knowledge. A minority student gets the runaround from the student aid office and decides to examine the incidence of federal loan programs to college students. A sophomore working at a local automobile factory realizes that many co-workers have come from or still have attachments to rural backgrounds, and he systematically finds out about their migration patterns. A waitress at a local health foods restaurant has knowledge about its suppliers and is able to use that as the basis of a new industry study. An antique streetcar buff goes through old trade magazines to put together a picture of the sources of technological change in light fixed-rail transportation and compares those causes with other arguments about the role of antitrust violations in displacing light fixed-rail urban transport. An American history major studies life in New England settlements to piece together a picture of income distribution in an earlier time.

The examples are legion, but one point is that, if you are free to choose your topic, you want to think about your strengths and experiences. Consider how they might relate to an analysis of some relevant economic problem or institution. What have you done? Where have you lived? Who do you know? The process is not easy. After all, a fish is probably unaware that it lives in water. It is difficult to isolate things and events that have surrounded you all your life, but they may be the seeds of an interesting paper.

There is another way you can make an original contribution. Much of empirical economics has emphasized statistical analysis of a few variables from rather large samples. This approach has the virtue of allowing economists to make general statements about economic behavior. Unfortunately, there are few case studies of specific situations and institutions. Yet, that is the way we often discover new mechanisms that we have never adequately understood or that we have never thought were important. You have an opportunity to do that kind of case study, whether it be in the field or in the library.

Finally, let us be realistic. You cannot always find an original subject, and sometimes the professor assigns the topic. Even in that situation, remember that the object of the exercise is to learn how to analyze and report the results clearly. Have you learned how to understand a problem, marshal evidence about it, and present your findings lucidly? Even if a thousand others have worked on the same topic, you have not, and because of your unique experiences, you may approach it just differently enough to enlighten even that know-it-all professor.

PICKING A QUESTION THAT WOULDN'T STRAIN THE RESOURCES OF THE FORD FOUNDATION TO ANSWER !

CHAPTER 3

How to find a topic

If the longest journey begins with a single step, it is also true that the first step is sometimes the hardest. In the writing of a term paper, that step is the selection of the topic —best described by the title of the paper.

Before you can choose the topic, the theme of the paper, you have to decide on the general area in economics within which the topic falls. Sometimes this decision is predetermined by the course. If you are assigned a term paper in a labor economics course, it is unlikely that the professor will be delighted to receive an essay on the role of barter exchange in medieval Europe. At other times, the topic may be constrained very little, if at all, by the instructor; for example, there may be many possibilities when you are assigned a paper in a principles of economics course.

There are numerous ways of distinguishing areas within economics. The traditional and now old-fashioned approach was to define economics as the production, distribution, consumption, and exchange of commodities. Thus, one distinguishes four subjects within the discipline. But this division is outdated and, in any event, too broad. Economics also has been separated into microeconomics and macroeconomics, in many respects a logical division, but again too broad to be useful.

What has evolved more recently are classification schemes relating to substantive areas of the economy, such as money and banking, labor, welfare, and industrial organization. These breakdowns read very much like titles of courses in a college catalog. One such schema, used by the *Journal of Economic Literature* (of which more will be said in chapter 8), is as follows:

000 General economics; Theory; History; Systems
  010 General economics
  020 General economic theory
  030 History of thought; methodology
  040 Economic history
  050 Economic systems

100 Economic growth; Development; Planning; Fluctuations

110 Economic growth; development; and planning theory and policy
120 Economic development studies
130 Economic fluctuations; forecasting; stabilization; and inflation

200 Quantitative economic methods and data
  210 Econometric, statistical, and mathematical

methods and models
220 Economic and social statistical data and analysis

300 Domestic monetary and fiscal
theory and institutions
310 Domestic monetary and
financial theory and
institutions
320 Fiscal theory and policy;
public finance

400 International economics
410 International trade theory
420 Trade relations; commercial policy; international
economic integration
430 Balance of payments;
international finance
440 International investment
and foreign aid

500 Administration; Business
finance; Marketing;
Accounting
510 Administration
520 Business finance and
investment
530 Marketing
540 Accounting

600 Industrial organization;
Technological change;

Industry studies
610 Industrial organization
and public policy
620 Economics of
technological change
630 Industry studies
640 Economic capacity

700 Agriculture; Natural resources
710 Agriculture
720 Natural resources
730 Economic geography

800 Manpower; Labor; Population
810 Manpower training and
allocation; labor force
and supply
820 Labor markets; public
policy
830 Trade unions; collective
bargaining; labor-
management relations
840 Demographic economics
850 Human capital

900 Welfare programs; Consumer
economics; Urban and
regional economics
910 Welfare; health; and
education
920 Consumer economics
930 Urban economics
940 Regional economics

The numbers before each heading or subheading are the classification code used as a shorthand reference to the area.

Suppose that you, the student, have chosen the area for your paper, or that the area has been selected for you. You then must choose the specific topic. Some professors assign these to students, sometimes providing a list of possibilities. In our courses, we have encouraged students to select their own and to be imaginative. A useful rule is to choose a topic that both interests you and is manageable. If the subject of inflation fascinates you, do not set out to compare the causes and consequences of inflation in 100 different countries during different periods. Perhaps you should restrict your study to the United States in the 1970s. Or you may want to compare inflation in the United States, Great Britain, Germany, and Japan during a certain period.

Another piece of advice is to act boldly. As Chairman Mao said: "Seize the day; seize the hour!" Perhaps allegations have been made that retail stores in poorer sections of your community charge higher prices than comparable stores in wealthy sections. That issue could serve as the theme of your paper.

As examples of specific topics, we list below the titles of all papers published in the first eight issues of the *M.S.U. Economist* (1971–1978). Before each title we indicate the classification code from the list given above. An asterisk indicates that the paper is published at the end of this volume. Authors' names are given in parentheses.

040 Poverty and the Distribution of Income and Wealth in Eighteenth-Century Suffolk County (John B. Palmer)*
050 The Nature of Chilean Socialism (John B. Palmer)
050 Regional Economic Development and Integration in the People's Republic of China (David P. Grunow)
120 Oil for the 1980s: Planning the Economic Development of Petroleum Reserves in Mexico (Eric M. Baxter)
130 Inflation in Britain since 1960 (Scott Bales)
130 The Causes and Consequences of the German Hyper-Inflation of 1918–1923 (Mark Murray)
220 An Analysis of Campaign Techniques Using the Logit Model (Elise L. Price)
310 An Evaluation of the 1968 Proposal to Reform the Discount Mechanism (Jeffrey Marquardt)
310 Regulation Q and the Prohibition against Paying Interest on Demand Deposits: Some Observations, Criticisms, and Recent Legislative Proposals (Scott W. Sievert)
320 An Annual Wealth Tax for the State of Michigan (Kevin J. Murphy)
320 The Lottery: Heads, I Win; Tails, You Lose (Michael P. Skirka)
320 The Michigan Single Business Tax: An Analysis of Equity, Efficiency, Stability, and Growth (Gerald Merrill)

410 The Brain Drain: Issues and Approaches (Laura Tavormina)

410 Stability in the Foreign-Exchange Market: A Comment (Mark J. Machina)

420 Log Export Restrictions (Richard Craswell)*

420 Trade Preferences and Developing Countries (E. G. Cunningham)

440 The Little Countries' Big Brother and His BOP Problem, or the Aid John Hannah Gives (Leslie V. Starr)

630 Freight Transport and Interstate Commerce Commission Regulation of Railroads (Julie A. Caswell)

630 The Gasoline Shortage: Supply and Demand in Long-Run and Short-Run Analysis (Larry Herman)

630 The Structural Change in the American Brewing Industry (Joseph A. Kirch)

630 A Survey of Price Discrimination among Lansing Area Food Prices (James M. Simmons)

720 The Economic Effects of Billboard Control (Brant Freer and Ronald Sutton)*

720 A Study of the Red Cedar River and the Effect of Government Action in the Control of Water Pollution (Belinda March)

830 Collective Bargaining and Michigan Teachers' Salaries: Adaption and Testing of a Static Salary Determination Model (Edward S. Cavin)

910 Allocation of Resources in the Lansing School District (Martin Lowy)

910 An Analysis of the Demand for Illicit Marijuana in a University Community and Projections for the Results of a Tax on Legalized Marijuana (Christopher Mallin)*

910 A Case Study of the Participation of the Poor in the Lansing Community Mental Health Center, or Why Wait until Johnny Gets His Gun? (Paul R. Baranek)

910 Compromise in Health Delivery Regulation: The PSRO Example (Linda L. Oleksyk)

910 Economic Analysis of Six Proposals to Improve Health Care Distribution (Bryan J. Dunlop)

910 The Economics of Heroin Addiction in Detroit and Its Consequences for the Poor (Joseph Connors)

910 Medicaid and the Emergency Room (John S. MacDonald)*

910 The Supplemental Security Income–Circuitbreaker–Alert Program of 1974 in St. Louis, Mo.: A Case Study of the Diversion of Federal Funds Intended for the Poor to the Middle and Working Classes (Daniel E. McGuire)

930 The Increased Price to Students of Living Closer to the University (Craig Weaver)*

930 Relocating the Poor—A Study of I-496 (Robert J. Dennis)

930 A Study of the Relationship between External Diseconomies and Population (Christine Schneider Schafer and Daniel Watson)*

CHAPTER 4

Choosing a strategy; accident favors the prepared mind; being flexible

You now have your topic, whether you have chosen it yourself or it has been assigned to you. The next decision concerns the approach, method, or technique that you are to use. What type of paper will it be?

One type concentrates on a review of the literature. A description and evaluation of a book in the field—that is, a book review—is the simplest paper of this kind. A more comprehensive approach is to review an array of material, ranging from books to journal articles. Obviously, this may require considerable work in your college library. Chapter 8 provides information on how to use the library to prepare a bibliography, that is, a collection of printed material, for a specific topic.

A second kind of paper is an essay, or "thinkpiece." The objective is to present your own views on an issue. This approach often means offering some comments or suggestions on a policy issue. The topic may also be theoretical: You develop or extend a model of economic behavior, which may or may not have implications for public policy. Usually, but not always, such models are best expressed in mathematical and/or geometrical terms.

The third type of paper is empirical in nature. The goal is to test a theoretical hypothesis by obtaining actual data and observing how well they fit the theory. Either time-series or survey data may be used. Time-series information is gathered over time (for example, observations may be annual, monthly, or weekly) and is printed in statistical publications. Chapter 10 describes how to find these. Survey data are not so readily available. You probably would have to obtain this material on your own, through interviews with individuals, households, firms, or government agencies. Some suggestions on obtaining and using survey data are provided in chapter 9. Statistical analysis, whether using time-series or survey data, and the use of computers and calculators are discussed in chapter 10.

Of course, a paper may combine aspects of two or even all three approaches. For example, a review of at least some of the literature is a good way to begin any paper. Even if you decide against a formal review of past work, reading the views of others or the results of their research is an ideal way of beginning to develop your own strategy.

How can you decide what type of paper your contribution should be? Should it be predominantly a review of the relevant literature, an essay, or an empirical study? Sometimes the choice is determined by your topic. If you want to examine varying grocery prices among the neighborhoods in your community, the best strategy is to assemble the survey data (the price information) yourself—unless, of course, you discover that another researcher has obtained the data in a form accessible to you. Statistical analysis then obviously follows.

Often, however, the choice of approach is a matter of your own preference. Consider a topic on the effect of the money supply on inflation. You may want to review the literature on this issue. Or you may want to build on the literature by developing or extending an existing theory of this inflationary process. Or you may consult a statistical publication to obtain data on the money supply and inflation for a given country during a certain period and test for a stable relationship between the two variables. Any combination of these approaches is also in order.

CHAPTER 5

*Breaking down the problem into small,
sequential tasks with intermediate deadlines*

After you have decided on your topic and approach, the
magnitude of the task facing you may seem overwhelming.

How do you start to prepare the paper? What should you do first?

We strongly suggest that you *plan* each stage of your work. Break down the problem of producing the paper into small, manageable tasks. Set a deadline for each task, and make every effort to follow this schedule.

It is almost impossible to write any paper without some idea of existing work on the topic. Your first task should be to obtain information on the "state of the art" in the subject you are investigating. One source of information is your professor or any other person knowledgeable in the topic. The customary and usually most reliable sources, however, are published works. Find the relevant printed material. Your campus library is the ideal place to begin. Information on how to use the library for this purpose is given in chapter 8.

For a survey paper, that is, a review of the literature, begin by reading the various published studies and then determine the main concepts running through them. This task requires some time and thought. Next, do some rereading with these concepts in mind. Ask how the authors differ from one another in their analyses. How are they similar? A poor survey simply reports what authors have written; a good survey points out common themes and compares and contrasts various authors' views.

You may make your survey paper even more impressive by extending your review of the literature (or of only one book) into a thinkpiece. Use the authors' analyses and views, as well as your own ideas about them, to make some original contributions. Perhaps you can develop a new implication for public policy or elaborate on an existing theory.

Preparation of a thinkpiece is similar to that for a survey paper, but the relative weight given the review of the literature and your own views is reversed. You must devote considerable time to developing your own thoughts, and the work of others is relevant only to the extent that it aids in this process.

Concerning the third type of papers, those empirically oriented, it is easy to plan a stream of sequential tasks. First, you must decide on the theory to be tested. Some background reading will be necessary. Second, you must collect the data, and you may have to consult the library for possible sources. Chapter 10 describes some sources of quantitative information and tells you how to go about finding others. Third, you must compute certain statistics from the data in order to test whether the theory is supported by the evidence you have assembled. These computations may be performed by hand, with small electronic calculators, or at the computer center on your campus. Fourth, you must interpret and evaluate the statistical results and decide whether the theory should be accepted or rejected on the basis of your test. In chapter 10 we provide some guidelines for constructing and interpreting statistics and offer a few comments on the use of calculators and computers.

YOU CAN'T TELL IT LIKE IT IS IF YOU DON'T UNDERSTAND IT

CHAPTER 6

Analysis, description, opinion, and emotion

Most of us have had the experience of asking someone how or why a thing works and getting a long involved answer which makes absolutely no sense. Perhaps you have had that experience with some of your professors. Perhaps they have had such experiences with you or some of your friends. Sometimes the explanation makes no sense because you do not know enough about the subject to understand it. Just as often, the person explaining it may not have a very clear grasp of the subject. What should you do? Do not be impressed by someone using big words who sounds authoritative. Ask questions until you are sure you *both* understand the explanation.

In writing a good term paper, the same sort of behavior is required. You have to ask questions and track down answers. Often, you cannot just ask someone; you must figure things out for yourself until the whole process seems simple, or at least clear. Until you reach that point in your research, you are not ready to stop, and you are not ready to write anything. Sometimes you can fool people with jargon and big words, but as P.T. Barnum might have said, you can fool some of your professors all the time, and all of your professors some of the time, but you can't fool all your professors all the time. You should be able to explain (to yourself or a roommate) the main mechanism behind the problem you are researching. If there are gaps that cannot be closed, do not ignore them. They may be important discoveries. For centuries, mathematicians tried to draw a square and a circle with the same area using only a straightedge and a compass. The breakthrough came when someone had the genius to ask whether it could be done and proved that it could not. Sometimes negative results are more important than positive results.

There are four words that often confuse students. If you can keep them straight, you are on your way to writing good research papers. They are *analysis, description, opinion,* and *emotion.*

Analysis means breaking something complex into its simple elements, tracing things to their sources, discovering principles underlying what you observe. It is hard to do, but once you have done it, you can say you understand. When you are writing an economics term paper, you have economic theory to help you understand how things work. Indeed, a good paper often consists only of showing how a simple theory does or does not explain some phenomenon.

For example, let us say you have collected data on prices charged by grocery stores in various neighborhoods. You have only described the prices, not analyzed them, and that does not constitute a good paper. Analysis consists of explaining why and how prices vary. Fortunately, you do not have to invent the wheel. You can begin to classify causes into demand factors (the choices buyers have, and their income) and supply (or cost) factors. Are stores in poor neighborhoods charging more or less than stores elsewhere for the same products? If more, then that has to be explained (assuming that you have taken quality differences into account). Are the stores in poor neighborhoods smaller, making economies of scale a factor? Are insurance, labor, capital, or other costs more expensive per unit of sales? If so, why? Are the sizes of purchases smaller? Are the stores faced with less competition and therefore can extract monopoly profit? These are all simple questions that your principles of economics course helps you to ask. You may find yourself dissatisfied with the standard explanations and may discover others as you probe the problem.

Description involves listing or reporting elements of a process or behavior without dissecting it or showing causal connections. For example, welfare departments have enormously complex rules for giving out payments. Simply stating those rules is a description. Showing how they fit into a standard negative income tax formula may explain that some of the variation is due to worries about work incentives and that various changes in payments are designed to give workers extra income. Description must precede analysis. You must know what you are trying to explain, but that is only the first step.

Opinion and **emotion** are quite different from analysis and description. When students are told they are supposed to do their own analysis, they often think that means they are being asked to express their opinion on a subject or to tell how they feel about a situation. Emotions and opinions are crucial in determining what is an important problem and in deciding, once you understand something, how to go about changing it. For example, to say that "grocers are ripping off the poor and I think it's terrible" is not a research paper. You must show that the prices vary in a particular way and that they are due to particular causes which you perceive through some theory derived from neoclassical economics, Marxist analysis, or perhaps just "common sense" about how things happen. Once you understand how the pricing takes place, then you might want to take a stand and develop a policy to change things based on that understanding.

Having a theory to help you in your search for the answer to a problem forces you to sit down at the start of your research and think things out. Figure out what the actors are trying to accomplish. Decide how they would be making their choices if they were rational. Try to guess who the conflicting parties are; try to find their interests. This process takes some time, but it actually *saves* you time in the long run. You will not have to take notes on all sorts of unnecessary material, and you will not get sidetracked. You can focus on those things that either confirm or refute your theories. You will know what to look for, what is relevant. Discovering how the pieces of the puzzle fit together is no accident; it takes a systematic and prepared mind.

FACTS,
TRUE FACTS,
AND FALSE
FACTS

CHAPTER 7

Types of evidence

It used to be said that the major weekly news magazines would write articles in the following way. Editors would sit down and write a story taking some particular perspective. They would leave blanks at appropriate places, and a large research staff would then fill in the blanks with facts that would support the story line. That is one reason why such magazines may not be good sources for your papers, but there is another message here. People are often enormously impressed with numbers and other data that appear to make a story believable. If someone is writing about the U.S. oil industry and sprinkles a few numbers around, such as the n-million barrels of oil we will import next year or the x-million cubic feet of gas we can ship across the country, people may accept the numbers as true and relevant; they may believe the author knows what he or she is talking about, even when the discussion goes beyond the numbers. A number that sounds precise is rarely questioned. But the requirements for evidence are much higher for academic projects, and it is important that you recognize that most "facts" are not facts, and those that are may be irrelevant.

There are many different kinds of facts. *There are twelve inches in a foot* is a fact which holds true by definition. *The speed of light is 186,000 miles per second* is a fact until someone measures it more accurately and finds the present figure incorrect — or that it cannot be measured. At least in the latter case one could clearly describe the process the physicist would use. Social and economic facts are much more slippery, and not just because observations frequently are very inaccurate. (On the latter point, see Oskar Morgenstern, *On the Accuracy of Economic Observations* [Princeton, N.J.: Princeton University Press, 1963].)

Often, a lot of *assuming* goes into an economic "fact." Consider the statement (from the U.S. Bureau of the Census) that 10 percent of American families are poor. A number of questions can be asked about such a seemingly precise statement. First, how does the Census Bureau define *family?* For example, does the term include all people living in the same housing unit, even nonrelatives? Second, how does the Census Bureau define *poverty?* It is, in actuality, an appallingly arbitrary business, with data from all sorts of surveys being mixed together in various ways. Obviously, given the same income, a large family is closer to the poverty line than a small one. Third, how does the Census Bureau define the actual income of individuals in comparison with the poverty level? Does income include hot lunches in schools? Vegetables grown in a garden? Imputed rents on housing? Capital gains? Fourth, who provides the information on income, and how accurate is it? Do people lie? Are the people interviewed representative?

You should be skeptical of economic facts that you find in quite respectable places. You have to figure out what the "facts" are supposed to measure, and how they are calculated. But that is only the first step. You then must figure out how to analyze and present such facts. This is what your statistics course was about, but sometimes the problem is not simple. One little book you might profitably read is Darrell Huff's *How to Lie with Statistics* (New York: W. W. Norton & Co., 1954).

We cannot reproduce a statistics course here, but we do want to mention a few matters.

Selection Bias. You always need to know how representative your sources are. They may have a selfish interest in giving incorrect information. Even if the data are accurate, they may come from an atypical part of the population. A classic example occurred recently at Michigan State University. There was a statewide election to determine whether 18-year-olds would be allowed to drink alcoholic beverages. The student newspaper conducted a survey in the university area and predicted that the law would pass overwhelmingly. In fact, the voters rejected it overwhelmingly. Obviously, the university community was not representative of all the voters in the state!

Fairness. Selecting the statistics to present involves a commitment to fairness. Growth rates are a good example. When the base number is small, small increases can be made to sound large if stated as rates of increase. Let us say you open a business, and 20 people buy your product the first day, 30 people the next. You can say that ten more people bought your products or that the rate of growth of customers was 50 percent in just one day. Both statements are correct, but the second may be misleading. Similar questions arise about measures of central tendency of distribution. Let us say that there are nine people with incomes of $3,000 per year and one person with an income of $33,000 per year. The median income (arrived at by dividing the population of ten people in half) is $3,000 per year. The average income (arrived at by dividing the total incomes by ten) is twice that. Which is more representative of income in the community? Perhaps you need to present evidence (such as the Gini coefficient) on the variance of the distribution as well. In any case, the median is less sensitive than the average to the effect of extreme observations.

Elaborate Tools. The availability of computer programs and even preprogrammed calculators has given students access to some powerful statistical techniques. Often, students can put data into a "canned" program and get all sorts of fancy numbers. In general, we advise students not to use techniques with which they are not familiar. It is better to present a table of averages than to report a lot of regression statistics that you do not understand. Of course, if you do understand them, by all means use the tools you have picked up. But if you have any doubts about the meaning of a statistic, it is not going to help you in your analysis, and you would do better to operate on your own level of understanding.

Numbers. Numbers have little meaning by themselves, even if they seem impressively large. Numbers need to be compared to determine whether they are large or growing. Furthermore, the comparisons that you undertake should always make a point about your central hypothesis. Unnecessary numbers will only bore or confuse people. For example, 10 million barrels of oil per day are relatively unimportant if world production is a trillion barrels daily and the United States uses 250 million barrels a day. If this country used fewer than 30 million barrels, then 10 million would be a large proportion of U.S. consumption.

Presentation. Supporting your paper with figures is an excellent idea. Numbers both provide a factual basis for and lend authority to your arguments. However, statistical information will improve your paper only if used sensibly. For example, one poor habit that even professional economists have is to give numbers more digits than are necessary. Let us say you are studying the effect of family income on gasoline consumption. If you write that a $1,000 increase in income implies an additional $51.34 spent on gasoline, you are overstating the findings. A more honest statement would be $51 (or even $50); the number is surely not accurate to the cent!

Often (although not always — see the comments on fairness, above), numbers are better stated in terms of percentages than in absolute figures. Generally, it is easier for the reader to grasp percentages than numbers in their original units. For example, if an industry's sales increased from $10 million last year to $11 million this year, it is probably more meaningful to describe the situation as a 10 percent increase in sales. Again referring to the example of U.S. oil consumption, if 10 million barrels are imported daily, and 50 million barrels are consumed, then imports provide 20 percent of

Chapter 7
29

daily consumption. The 20 percent figure almost certainly best describes the point that you want to make.

FINDING OUT WHAT'S KNOWN
EVEN WHEN IT'S WRONG

CHAPTER 8

*How to do library research, including
books, journals, documents, and newspapers*

For almost any term paper, some library work is essential.
You must develop a bibliography of items (books, journal
articles, and so forth) for use in your paper and then borrow
them from a library. Often these books or articles will cite

other works on the same topic, and these should be added to your bibliography.

Let us consider the problem of finding and obtaining materials once their titles are known. Compile your bibliographical list of books (by author and title), journals, and newspapers (by titles of the periodicals in which articles you want were published). Go to the card catalog of your campus library. This is an index of the library's holdings, each of which (books, periodicals, pamphlets, and so forth) has a card that lists author or editor, title, publisher, and the item's call number. The latter is an alphabetical and numerical filing code that enables you or the library staff to find the item on the library's shelves. If some of the items in your bibliography are not in your library's holdings (there is no entry in the card catalog), try to obtain them through the interlibrary loan service.

Card catalogs typically arrange the library's holdings alphabetically by author and/or title, so it is an easy matter to find the call numbers of your bibliographical material. Copy the call numbers of all items and use these (together with a map of your library showing where materials with those call numbers are located) to fetch the desired books and periodicals. (Some libraries permit only staff members to enter the stacks.) Generally, libraries allow books to be checked out for a reasonable time. However, many do not permit journals to be checked out, or only for brief periods. You may read the articles within the library, or reproduce them and take the copies elsewhere to study. (Such reproduction is regulated by copyright laws. For example, you cannot legally reproduce an article and sell copies to others. Generally, reproduction for one's own scholarly purposes is permitted.) Except for recent issues, newspapers usually are available only on microfilm. If your library has a microfilm collection, it will also have machines that magnify the film, enabling you to find and read the issues in which your bibliographical articles appeared. The library may also have a special microfilm reader/copier, one that can reproduce selected newspaper pages. This machine is especially useful, as it can be inconvenient to take notes while reading a microfilm.

As mentioned earlier, the first step in preparing a term paper is to develop a bibliography. Depending on your topic and the approach chosen, the amount of bibliographical work may vary from very little to about half of your total effort on the paper. Only some of the information that follows will be useful for any particular paper.

It is a good idea to begin by consulting some relevant reference works. These special publications provide an indexed guide to the literature in specific areas. Under various subject headings, they list authors, titles, and publication information (book date and publisher; journal name, volume, and page numbers; newspaper issue and page numbers). More than one subject heading may relate to your topic. Usually, these headings are in alphabetical order; in some cases they are so short that the reader can scan the entries and select the appropriate category or categories. For example, the classification scheme shown in chapter 3 is used by the *Journal of Economic Literature* to arrange its listing of books in economics.

It is always a good idea to read a reference work's description of its classification system. Different works can vary greatly. For example, newspaper indexes are extremely detailed, while the classification system of the *Journal of Economic Literature* for articles is an extension of its scheme for books. Consider the classification number 440 (International investment and foreign aid) used for books. In the case of articles, this classification is divided into three headings:

441 International investment and capital markets
442 International business
443 International aid

Generally, reference works provide not only subject indexes but also author indexes, the latter listing all works by a given author published before the reference work went to press.

One source of information is an encyclopedia. The subject index in these books refers to entries within the encyclopedia itself, and/or the entries are arranged alphabetically according to subject heading. General encyclopedias (such as the *Encyclopedia Britannica* and *Encyclopedia Americana)* may provide factual information for your paper, depending on the topic. But more useful, because of its analytical approach, is the *International Encyclopedia of the Social Sciences,* a 17-volume work published in 1968. Some earlier encyclopedias of this type are the *Encyclopedia of the Social Sciences,* published in the 1930s, and *Palgrave's Dictionary of Political Economy,* which originally appeared in the 1890s. These last two are excellent but are of value today mainly for historical material. Because even the *International Encyclopedia* is somewhat outdated, it cannot be a substitute for consulting more recent literature on your topic.

Most economists would agree that the best newspapers in the United States for economic reporting and commentary are the *New York Times* and the *Wall Street Journal.* Other possible sources are the *Washington Post, National Observer,* and *Christian Science Monitor.* All of these publish individual indexes of their articles (*New York Times Index, Wall Street Journal Index*), except for the *Washington Post,* which is indexed along with several other newspapers in the Bell & Howell *Newspaper Index.* The *New York Times Index* is especially useful, because the entries themselves provide an abstract of the news. For factual information of a nonstatistical nature, these major newspapers are often the best source.

What about indexes of articles in scholarly economics journals? The best one is the *Index of Economic Articles in Journals and Collective Volumes* (formerly called the *Index of Economic Journals*). This publication indexes journals back to 1886. Earlier volumes cover several years of literature, and the first seven volumes run through 1965. Thereafter, each volume is devoted to one year. This annual index is coordinated with the *Journal of Economic Literature* (*JEL*), and the subject index is an expansion of the *JEL*'s three-digit classification system to a four-digit system.

The *Index of Economic Articles* is always several years behind in its publication. Fortunately, the *JEL*, a quarterly, provides up-to-date indexing of articles in economics journals. It also offers short abstracts of some of these articles. If the final volume available in the *Index of Economic Articles* pertains to the year 1978, for example, you should consult issues of the *JEL* covering 1979, 1980, and so on.

Of interest primarily to specialists is the *International Bibliography of Economics* (1952–   ). Its virtues are the large number of journals indexed and the coverage given to publications in non-English languages.

Several reference works index not only articles that appear in economics journals but also those published in journals specific to other social sciences. If your paper is an interdisciplinary study, you may wish to consult these indexes. Noteworthy is the *Social Sciences Index* (1974–   ), an offshoot of the *Social Sciences and Humanities Index* (1965–1973), itself a successor to the *International Index* (1907–1965). More extensive in journals covered are the *Public Affairs Information Service Bulletin* (1915–   )

and the *Social Sciences Citation Index* (1969-   ). The
latter is especially useful because of its original indexing
schemes. Its permuterm (permutation + term) index is a
refined subject index in which all significant word pairs in
the title of an article serve as subject headings. Its citation
index lists the previously published items (books, articles,
theses, or any other kind of publication) referred to in current articles.

If your paper is oriented toward business as such, then
several indexes will be of use. Articles that appear in
business journals (those specializing in such fields as accounting, advertising, banking and finance, insurance, and
marketing) are indexed in the *Business Periodicals Index*
(1958-   ), an offshoot of the *Industrial Arts Index*
(1913-1957). More oriented to specific industries, companies, and products are the *F & S Index of Corporations
and Industries* (1960-   ), for U.S. corporations, and the
F & S Index International, for foreign companies. These
Funk & Scott indexes cover periodicals of many kinds, including journals, newspapers, financial reports, and various
trade publications. The annual *Bibliography of [year]
Publications of University Bureaus of Business and
Economic Research* (1956-   ) indexes publications
(books, monographs, periodicals, working papers, and
bulletins) of colleges of business in various universities. This
is a desirable service because such publications rarely appear
in broader indexes.

How about finding books—as distinct from journal articles and other periodical information—for your
bibliography? If you have carefully surveyed the journal
literature, then you need consult, at the most, only recent
issues of reference works that index books on your topic. The
reason is that the articles will almost invariably contain
references to the prominent books on your subject. (And

these books will cite other, perhaps less prominent, books in the field; and so on. But relax, the process *does* have an ending.)

A good source of information on newly published books is the *Journal of Economic Literature.* This journal not only classifies such books but also annotates (that is, briefly describes) their contents. Furthermore, selected books are given book reviews, separately classified. (Other scholarly journals in economics review books, but do not classify their reviews.) The *Economic Journal*, a quarterly British publication, also classifies and annotates new books. Its descriptions are more evaluative than those in the *Journal of Economic Literature.*.

Collective volumes (such as conference papers, collected essays, proceedings, and books of readings) in economics are indexed in the *Index of Economic Articles in Journals and Collective Volumes.* Coverage began in 1960, and collective volumes are selected from the books annotated in the *JEL.*

A comprehensive classification and annotation of economics books in the English language is provided in the quarterly *Economic Books: Current Selections.* Under various titles (*International Economics Selections Bibliography, Series 1: New Books in Economics; Economics Library Selections, Cumulative Bibliography Series 1 and 2, 1954–1962*), this service dates back to 1954.

Books, pamphlets, government publications, and other printed matter — in addition to articles in journals — are indexed in the *International Bibliography of Economics* and the *Public Affairs Information Service Bulletin.* As mentioned earlier, the coverage extends beyond economics to other social sciences. Business books are indexed in *Business Books in Print* (1973-   ), which is restricted to U.S. publications.

Very important sources of information, whether factual, statistical, or analytical, are the numerous and varied publications of the federal government. In many libraries, these are kept in a separate collection along with other government or public documents, that is, publications issued by U.S. governmental units (whether federal, state, or local), foreign governments, and international organizations (United Nations, International Monetary Fund, and so forth).

The standard index for documents issued by all branches and agencies of the federal government is the *Monthly Catalog of United States Government Publications* (1895-   ). The December issue provides an annual index. The *Cumulative Subject Index of the Monthly Catalog of United States Government Publications, 1900–1971,* issued by a private publisher, also is invaluable. The *Public Affairs Information Service Bulletin*, already mentioned twice, provides selective indexing of government publications. The *Congressional Information Service Index to Publications of the United States Congress* (1970-   ) is a monthly guide to congressional documents, useful because of its comprehensiveness and the abstracts it provides.

We have mentioned the major reference works available. There are other indexes and guides to the types of materials emphasized here and to additional publications (for example, those of state and local governments, foreign governments, and international organizations). For information on these and for further detail on the reference works discussed here, the serious scholar should consult one or more of the bibliographical sources described below.

John Fletcher, ed., *The Use of Economics Literature* (Hamden, Ct.: Archon Books, 1971), provides excellent information and advice on conducting economics research, with particular attention to preparing bibliographies. There are individual chapters on periodicals, unpublished material, British government publications, U.S. government publications, and international organizations' documents, as well as a dozen chapters on conducting research in individual fields within economics (such as agricultural economics, labor economics, and public finance). The American reader should be aware of the book's British orientation.

William A. Katz, *Introduction to Reference Work. Volume I. Basic Information Sources,* 2d ed. (New York: McGraw-Hill, 1974), has useful chapters on encyclopedias and government documents, as well as other topics.

Eugene P. Sheehy, *Guide to Reference Books,* 9th ed. (Chicago: American Library Association, 1976), pp. 497–531, provides a list, with short descriptions, of bibliographical guides (indexes, dictionaries, encyclopedias, atlases, and directories) in economics and various business fields.

C. R. Goeldner and Laura M. Dirks, "Business Facts: Where to Find Them," *MSU Business Topics* 24 (Summer 1976):23–36, assembles two useful lists of information sources with a business orientation. One list provides sources of primary data and statistical information (government publications, trade publication statistical issues, and business guides and services). The other cites general reference sources of business information and ideas (indexes, periodicals and periodical directories, bibliographies and special guides, trade associations, and other basic sources).

IT'S OK TO TALK TO STRANGERS

CHAPTER 9

*How to conduct an
interview or take a survey*

Some things cannot be looked up in books or found in documents. You often must go out and gather information yourself. That means conducting an interview, and doing that well is a remarkably useful skill. Depending on the information you need, questions occasionally can be reduced to a short page which respondents can fill out themselves. At other times, you must sit down with your source for several in-depth sessions.

The most complete and authoritative guide we know on interview methods for obtaining economic information is John B. Lansing and James N. Morgan, *Economic Survey Methods* (Ann Arbor: Survey Research Center, Institute for Social Research, University of Michigan, 1974). Our discussion centers around several key questions.

What are you trying to find out?

The cost to you of doing a survey is your time, and the cost to your respondents is their time. You should pose a few clear questions precisely aimed at your problem so that you do not waste your time or theirs. Some people will answer innumerable vague questions without complaint, but most will not put up with such incompetence and need to be convinced that you know what you are doing. Asking clear questions that require limited answers also helps you to analyze responses. You need to think carefully about your questions, and you should try them out on others to see if they interpret them the same way you do.

Avoid biasing your results by asking loaded questions. The following are examples: "Don't you think it's awful the way the welfare department treats you?" "Right thinking people have agreed that this is silly; what do you think?" It is not unusual for advertising agencies and interest groups to ask questions in such a way that the answer they want is returned, but you cannot use such techniques if you want reliable information.

One of the important differences between economic and other types of questionnaires is that you usually want to measure *behavior* rather than attitudes or opinions.

Economists also try to avoid questions about what people would do in certain situations. Instead, they prefer to see how different kinds of behavior are related to actual circumstances. For example, you could ask people whether they think public transportation is a good idea. You are asking their opinion in a rather open-ended and almost meaningless way. To be more precise, you could ask whether they would take the bus if it ran within two blocks of their home and the ride cost 50 cents. You are still posing a "what if" situation. The best course might be to ask individuals whether or not they take the bus. Using other data you collect from them, you then might try to determine whether the bus is related to convenience and cost (including time) factors facing particular respondents.

Who are you studying?

The proper unit of analysis is not always obvious. You cannot talk to everyone, so you must select a sample. The question is, what is the population from which you choose? Sampling different groups will provide answers to different questions. For example, if you want to know about usage of a campus bus system, you can talk only to bus riders, or you can talk to a sample of students, some of whom ride buses and some of whom do not. Bus riders can answer questions about the quality of the bus service and about how their frequency of bus usage varies. The more general population can tell you about the decision to ride the bus or use other forms of transportation. You need to consider the choices facing particular groups. It is only from among those choices that the group can select, and you can analyze only that group's selection process.

What are the causal variables?

In addition to selecting the economic variable or behavior to be explained, you need to ask questions about the variables or factors which you think influence that behavior. Rarely can you go back and ask some question you overlooked. That means you must think in advance about the possible causes. Usually, there are economic variables (such as price, income, and quality of service) and demographic characteristics (such as age and sex) that may account for differences in tastes or circumstances of the respondents. To sort all this out, you need to frame some hypotheses before you design your questionnaire. A *hypothesis* is an analytical statement, that is, a statement about a causal mechanism, and it will be accepted or rejected depending on the results of your questionnaire (or other empirical investigation). Let us say you are surveying apartment rents. If you think that size of unit and distance from some central place affect price, then you have to ask about price, distance, and size. Of course, you may not need to ask about distance, but can figure that out yourself from information you record on the location of each apartment. After you have taken the survey and processed the data, you can decide the extent to which your hypotheses are supported by your investigation.

What strategy should be used for selecting your sample?

Even after deciding on the population you are studying, it is not always easy to choose a representative sample. You must be careful in selecting the people who will answer your questions. For example, using a student telephone directory to survey freshmen may yield a biased sample if some do not have telephones and if the lack of a telephone is systematically related to the variables you are trying to explain.

You may need to stratify your sample to make sure you get enough of a certain kind of observation. *Stratification* means that you separate the elements in the population by relevant group (for example, men and women if you are interested in the effect of sex on occupation or income; or different income classes if your objective is to investigate the savings habits of households). Stratifying your sample often requires a conscious effort; it does not happen naturally. For example, if you are comparing minority and nonminority student aid, you must have an ample number of minority students in your sample, even though, by definition, they will be harder to find.

To avoid biased results, it is often a good idea to choose your sample "at random." (When stratification is used, random sampling applies to each sample subgroup.) If you are investigating gasoline prices in a city, do not confine yourself to self-serve stations; that would understate prices. If there are 100 gasoline stations in your city, and you have time and resources to visit only five, a way to accomplish random sampling would be to assign each station a number, place the numbers in a hat (one paper for each number), shake it well, and draw five numbers; these will be the stations you will visit. Another way to accomplish random sampling is by the use of random-number tables, found and explained in almost any statistics textbook.

How will you collect your data?

A major step in data collection is designing a form and deciding how it will be administered. Often, this latter means some acting on your part. If you want to talk with bank loan officers about redlining, you may need to dress and speak in a way that will gain their cooperation.

In designing the questionnaire—whether to be completed and returned by mail or administered by you—several rules should be followed. First, ask only relevant questions. Do not request information that you will not use. Second, multiple-choice selections (for example, yes/no or always/often/sometimes/rarely/never) or questions involving a quantitative answer (for example, the number of times a week someone rides the bus) are better than open-ended questions, both for ensuring responses and in aiding your processing of the answers. However, you should allow respondents to elaborate on their answers if they wish. (This is both a means of ensuring your correct interpretation of the response and a matter of courtesy in hearing the person out.) Third, in a written questionnaire, confine the material to one page of neatly typed questions. This type of questionnaire is far more likely to be answered than an untidy one several pages long. To ensure return of the questionnaire, enclose a stamped self-addressed envelope. Fourth, when interviewing orally (whether by telephone or in person), allow respondents time to reflect on their answers before proceeding to the next question. Fifth, have respondents (or yourself) write answers in special boxes and reduce handwriting to a minimum; this ensures greater cooperation, saves time, and makes the forms easier to process when you analyze your collected data.

What etiquette should you follow?

Remember that the people you interview have their own lives to lead. If they grant you a personal interview or are willing to converse over the telephone (or if they complete a written questionnaire), they are doing you a favor. Take a minimum of their time, and before asking any questions tell them how much time you will require. Keep your questions brief and to the point. Whether you request an interview by telephone, by mail, or in person, be courteous. If the interview is by appointment, be on time. (Do not scold the interviewee if he or she is late!) Following the interview, a thank-you note provides a gracious touch. If the interviewed party might be interested in your findings (for example, a spokesperson for a business firm or a government official), you might also forward a copy of your completed paper.

An issue not often mentioned in textbooks is the ethics of confidentiality. When people tell you something in private, they often can be badly hurt if such information gets out. If you promise them confidentiality, then you have an obligation to protect your sources. You should design your questions so that the answers cannot be traced, and you should destroy the questionnaires after completing your analysis if there is anything at all confidential on them. Then neither you nor anyone else can use such information in a harmful way.

How will you present your data?

You want to use the appropriate statistical techniques to reduce your data to a few numbers that are easy to interpret. Often, this is best done by use of tables which show how mean or average values of your variables differ for groups in your sample. If you have a strong background in statistics, you might consider analysis of variance or regression techniques, but simple tests for the significance of differences in means (to be found in any introductory textbook on statistics) should be more than adequate if you have designed your survey well.

NUMBERS ARE REAL
AND IMAGINARY

CHAPTER 10

How to use statistics

If you write an empirical term paper, one that tests hypotheses statistically, you will have to obtain information on the variables or factors mentioned in the hypotheses. Unfortunately, there are few indexes to statistical sources. The most useful is the *American Statistics Index,* a comprehensive guide to the many statistical publications of the federal government. It is privately published annually, with monthly supplements. *Statistics Sources,* revised irregularly, indexes statistical material published by the U.S. government, foreign governments, and international organizations. Its limited coverage restricts its usefulness. *Sources of European Economic Information,* now in its second edition, discusses where to find economic data for 17 European countries. John Fletcher, ed., *The Use of Economics Literature* (Hamden, Ct.: Archon Books, 1971), is a valuable guide. Below, we list some major sources of statistical material.

The publications of the U.S. government are numerous. One of the most important is the *Statistical Abstract of the United States* (annual), an invaluable basic source of U.S. statistics of all kinds: economic, social, demographic, and so forth. It is published by the Bureau of the Census, which also issues the *Census of Manufacturers* and *Census of Business* at five-year intervals, both of which are confined to industry data. For long-term data of all kinds, *Historical Statistics of the United States, Colonial Times to 1970,* is an excellent source.

Many other countries issue annual statistical yearbooks, and some countries are the subject of an historical compendium volume; these latter are sometimes privately compiled and published. B. R. Mitchell, *European Historical Statistics 1750–1970* (New York: Columbia University Press, 1975), is especially valuable both because it compiles comparable historical data for many European countries (including the United Kingdom) and because it provides reference to the countries' official statistical yearbooks. Other historical compendia are Bank of Japan, *Hundred-Year Statistics of the Japanese Economy* (July 1966); Kazushi Ohkawa and Miyohei Shinohara, *Patterns of Japanese Economic Development: A Quantitative Appraisal* (New

Haven: Yale University Press, 1979); B. R. Mitchell and Phyllis Deane, *Abstract of British Historical Statistics* (Cambridge: the University Press, 1962); and M. C. Urquhart and K. A. H. Buckley, eds., *Historical Statistics of Canada* (Toronto: Macmillan Company of Canada, 1965).

Ongoing economic statistics of all kinds are published by the Office of Business Economics, U.S. Department of Commerce, in its monthly *Survey of Current Business* and biennial *Business Statistics*. Mainly macroeconomic data are also provided by the Council of Economic Advisers, *Economic Indicators* (monthly), and the Board of Governors of the Federal Reserve System, *Federal Reserve Bulletin*. Some regional Federal Reserve banks (such as those in St. Louis and San Francisco) also publish useful data, both national and regional. For state and local data, statistical abstracts exist for many states. For example, the *Michigan Statistical Abstract* is compiled and published annually by the Division of Research, Graduate School of Business Administration, Michigan State University.

Foreign governments issue much statistical information, but this will not be discussed here. Rather, we will mention some publications of international organizations; these provide data for all (or virtually all) members of the organization on an individual country basis. The United Nations Statistical Office publishes the *Statistical Yearbook*, supplemented by its *Monthly Bulletin of Statistics*. It issues several other annual compendia: *Yearbook of National Accounts Statistics*, *Yearbook of International Trade Statistics*, and *Demographic Yearbook*. The International Labour Office publishes the *Yearbook of Labour Statistics* and the quarterly *Bulletin of Labour Statistics*. Virtually all nations participate in these two organizations.

The International Monetary Fund has almost universal membership in the non-Communist world (the important nonmember being Switzerland). It publishes *International Financial Statistics* each month, with occasional supplements covering long periods, as well as *Balance of Payments Yearbook, Government Finance Statistics Yearbook,* and *Direction of Trade.*

Although its membership is restricted to 21 non-Communist industrial nations, the Organization for Economic Cooperation and Development (OECD) is an excellent source of information. Its members are among the most important countries in the non-Communist world (the United States, United Kingdom, Canada, Japan, Yugoslavia, Australia, New Zealand, and many Western European countries). The OECD issues much valuable statistical data in its monthly *Main Economic Indicators,* quarterly *Statistics of Foreign Trade,* and annual *National Accounts of OECD Countries, Labour Force Statistics, OECD Financial Statistics,* and *Statistics of Energy.*

Once you have obtained the data, they must be processed in order to test your hypotheses and thus be of value for your term paper. To learn about statistical techniques, you should consult a statistics textbook and, if possible, take at least one course in statistics. Graduate students in economics take courses in econometrics, which is a fancy name for statistics applied to economic data and hypotheses.

We discussed the use of statistics in chapters 7 and 9. Here, we confine ourselves to some words of caution. *Do not apply statistical techniques without thinking carefully about what you are doing.* Suppose you decide to compute the average of a variable with observations of, say, 2, 3, 4 and 60, 63, 72. The average is 34, but it is not a representative value; it hides rather than provides information in this case. There are two samples at hand, or, rather, the sample seems to emanate from two distinct populations. Look at your data before you leap to perform statistical computations with them.

How should you go about making computations? Small electronic calculators have become inexpensive and quite sophisticated. For many purposes, it is worth your while to purchase one, and it will surely be useful for an empirically oriented term paper. The small calculator cannot cope with involved statistical computations, however. For these you must consider using the facilities of your university's computer center. Remember that the computer is nothing more than a high-speed clerk. Computers are always *logical,* but they are only *reasonable* if you obey the rules of the program you decide to use. Be careful to punch your data and program cards carefully—indeed, *perfectly.* And check that your results make sense.

What about the presentation of statistics or other numerical data? Basically, there are three ways: tables, charts or graphs, and textual writing. When you have a *list* of numbers to show readers, it is tedious to read them in paragraphs. A table or chart provides a more effective and concise presentation. But when should a table be used and when a chart? Basically, a table is required when it is important to show exact numbers and when you want the reader to be able to consult individual items in the list. A chart is preferable when the *pattern* of the numbers (for example, a cycle or trend over time) is the important feature.

Do not put unimportant or trivial data in your tables or charts (of course, they should not go in the text, either). Too much information is as bad as too little. Do not swamp the reader with a multitude of numbers that you are too lazy to process into fewer bits of information. Nor should tables or charts be complicated. Often two or three *simple* tables are better than one involved table. Similarly, too many lines or curves on a single graph will confuse the reader.

Each table and chart should be numbered consecutively (Table 1, Table 2, and so on) and should have a brief descriptive title. The tables and charts may be referred to in the text by their numbers. Indeed, it is rare for a writer to include tables or charts without some reference to them in the written part of the paper. As a general rule, you should highlight the important points of any table or chart in the text. It should be possible for someone to read and understand your paper while ignoring any charts or tables; these need be consulted only for detail.

Sources of the data should be cited at the bottom of each chart or table. Footnotes may be added to clarify information, but we advise that these be used only sparingly. Unnecessary complication can ruin the main virtue of a table or chart, namely, ease of presentation. In the drawing of charts and graphs, there are many errors to be avoided, such as omitting the origin, failing to label components, and expressing variables in inappropriate units or not measuring them according to scale. Such mistakes can distort the graph or chart and mislead the reader. An excellent discussion of the principal pitfalls in graphical presentation in economics is found in William J. Baumol and Alan S. Blinder, *Economics: Principles and Policy* (New York: Harcourt Brace Jovanovich, 1979), pp. 27–35.

IF IT'S STRAIGHT
FROM THE HORSE'S MOUTH
YOU HAD BETTER
NAME THE HORSE

CHAPTER 11

*Avoiding plagiarism, preparing
footnotes and bibliographies*

You have heard the word *plagiarism*. Basically, it means
copying someone else's work without acknowledging the
original author. You also know that if someone is caught
plagiarizing, the penalty could range from failure in the
course to expulsion from college. Plagiarism is to be avoided
at all costs, and this is not difficult. When making notes, be

sure to indicate to yourself which words are taken directly
from the author. If you do not, it may be difficult later on to
tell the difference between what the book said and any ideas
you may have written down about the book. Many students
are confused about the boundaries between plagiarism and
paraphrasing. According to Webster's *Collegiate Dictionary,* a paraphrase is "a restatement of a text, passage, or
work giving the meaning in another form." The purpose is
to clarify or amplify the material you are discussing. But just
because you do not use an author's *exact* words does not
mean you are not plagiarizing. If you have any doubts, it is a
good idea to talk with your professor and be certain you
understand the definition of plagiarism as it is in your
college or university. Just remember that a direct quotation
always requires quotation marks (or indentation) and a reference note, and a paraphrase also may require a footnote
or other form of citation.

If you are using a direct quotation from a speech, book,
article, and so forth, somewhere in the same paragraph, tell
who the author is.

> John Dough said: "The black markets of the world
> thrive in spite of numerous governmental restrictions."

If the quotation goes on for several sentences, you could indent and single-space it without quotation marks.

Next, you want to tell where you found this important
statement. There are several ways to do so. One is to include
that information along with the reference to the author's
name: As John Dough said in *Memoirs of a Madman* (New
York: Puddlejumper & Co., 1949, p. 256). That method
can get a bit cumbersome, however. An easier way would be
to use a footnote. Place the number of the footnote immediately after the quotation or statement, like this.[1] Then,
depending on your preference or that of your professor,

place the single-spaced footnote, with the first line indented, at the bottom of the page or on a separate page of notes to appear at the end of the paper. In any case, the footnote would read:

[1]John Dough, *Memoirs of a Madman* (New York: Puddle-jumpers & Co., 1949), p. 256.

For a book with as many as three authors, list each one, the way they appear in the original work:

[2]John Dough, Jane Day, and Germaine Mark, *Inflationary Spiral* (New York: Spider Press, 1956), p. 78.

For four or more authors, you need list only the first one, followed by et al., and continue with the same form as above. Et al. is a Latin abbreviation meaning "and others." Increasingly, the practice is to use "and others" and to spell out all Latin abbreviations (use "for example" rather than e.g., "that is" rather than i.e., and "and so forth" rather than etc.).

If an author's book has been edited or translated by someone else, the following form applies, using either "ed." or "trans." when appropriate.

[3]William Arson, *Inflammatory Speeches,* ed. Percy Pushbottom (Boston: Baked Beans Press, 1972), p. 33.

When no author is given, only an editor, list the editor as you would the author, followed by a comma and "ed.,".

If the statements referred to come from one piece within a collection, use the following form:

[4]John Dough, "Trading Is Fun," in *Black Market Guidebook* (Philadelphia: Big Bucks Publishing Co., 1979), p. 225.

For periodicals, use the forms given below.
For a magazine article with a by-line:

[5]John Dough, "The Politics of Price Gouging," *Consumer Retorts,* January 1979, p. 13.

When no author is given for a magazine article:

[6]"The Failing Economy," *Oldweek,* 13 December 1972, p. 55.

For an article in a scholarly journal:

[7]John Dough, "The Future Is in Our Hands," *Journal of Farsighted Fellows* 42 (January 1959): 442-43.

Note that the volume number (42) and month (January) or season (winter) should be used.

Newspaper articles can be footnoted in two ways. For a small one-section paper, give the name of the newspaper and the date. For multisectioned newspapers, you must include the author's name (if given), the title of the article, the newspaper, date, section, and page.

[8]John Dough, "Dollar Rebounds in World Market," *New York Chimes,* 29 February 1976, sec. E, p. 5.

Depending on the nature of your topic, you may be using information gathered through interviews. This material should also be footnoted.

[9]Interview with Daddy Warbucks, National World Bank, New York, 7 June 1977.

A second reference to the same book or article once was a complicated process requiring the use of Latin abbreviations. Now, the Modern Language Association recommends including the second reference within the body of the paper. For example: American-made cars are expected to sell rapidly in Outer Mongolia in 1992 (Dough, p. 90), or (Dough, *Cars,* p. 90), to distinguish which of the many items by Dough you have cited previously. If the second reference is cited in the footnotes, use the author's last name, a shortened form of the title, and the page number.

The above list of suggested footnotes includes most of the forms you will need in the course of preparing your term paper. However, if you encounter a problem not explained here, you might want to consult *Student's Guide to Writing College Papers,* by Kate L. Turabian (Chicago: University of Chicago Press, 1976).

In addition to material presented in the body of the paper and duly footnoted, you may have some information you think might help the reader understand the topic more clearly. This information may be too lengthy for inclusion in the paper itself, or it may not be directly related to your main points. Maps, charts, graphs, and the full text of documents can be presented in appendices at the end of the paper. For each piece you will need a title, such as Appendix A, Appendix B, and so forth. You can refer to these in the body of the paper as: (See Appendix A). This material should be something you genuinely believe is relevant to the better understanding of your topic. Do not use an appendix to show the professor how many documents you examined or how well you can photocopy charts. Relevancy is the key here.

Another important part of your paper is the bibliography. It is distinct from footnotes because it is arranged alphabetically by author and gives the reader information about the body of work from which you derived your material. A footnote refers to specific areas within the works. The bibliography lists all your reference materials in one place — at the end of your paper.

Using the last names of the authors, followed by his or her first name or two initials, list the authors in alphabetical order, with the author's name flush left and succeeding lines indented. References are single-spaced, with double-spacing between each work. Usually, two or more publications by the same author are arranged chronologically, the most recent publication last.

Book by one author

Adams, J. D. *The Decline of the Dime*. New York: Nickel and Dime Press, 1954.

— — —. *The Decline of the Quarter*. New York: Nickel and Dime Press, 1963.

Book by two or more authors

Counter, Joseph, and Millie Millions. *The Need for a Balanced Budget*. Burlington, Iowa: Budget Books, 1979.

Book with a translator or editor

Diaz, Juan. *Letters of a Financier,* trans. Juanita Peso. Philadelphia: J. L. Banks Books, 1965.

Encyclopedia or dictionary reference, author given

Encyclopedia Columbiana. 3d ed. (1956–1957), s.v.* "Economics." By Sarah Smart.

Encyclopedia or dictionary reference, no author given

Factual Facts Dictionary. 1972 ed., s.v. "Financial Wizards."

Article with no author given

"Now Is the Time to Invest." *Money Magic Newsletter,* 20 September 1929, p. 45.

A group, association, or institution as author

Organization of American Banks. *Guide to Lending Laws*. Washington, D.C.: Organization of American Banks, 1971.

Sub verbo, or "under the word."

Article in scholarly journal

Price, Hy. "Projections for a Favorable Balance of Trade by
1990." *Journal of Educated Guesses* 42 (July 1960):
52-73.

Article in popular magazine,
author given

Porter, Carrie. "The Decline of Train Services." *Tracks
and Trains,* May 1970, pp. 48-53.

Government documents,
hearings, and reports

U.S. Congress. House. Ways and Means Committee. *Banking and Credit Card Relationships,* paper prepared for
the committee by Amerigo Expresso. Committee Study
Paper 50. Washington, D.C.: U.S. Government Printing
Office, 1978.

U.S. Congress. Senate. Committee on Labor and Unem-
ployment. *Fair Unemployment Act of 1979,* Report to
Accompany S. R. 7855. 93rd Cong., 2d sess., 1980.
S. Rept. 245.

U.S. Constitution. Art. I, sec. 1.

U.S. Department of Commerce. *Rate Schedules for Non-
existent Routes.* Department of Commerce Pamphlet no.
2, by I. M. Truckin. Washington, D.C.: U.S. Government Printing Office, 1966.

U.S. Department of Health, Education and Welfare. *Report on Education in Alaskan Igloo Schools.* Rural Education Series, no. 77. 1967. Washington, D.C.: Department of Health, Education and Welfare.

There may be other types of references you would have to
include in your bibliography, but those listed above should
suffice for most economics term papers. If you do not find

the form you require here, refer to the book by Kate L. Turabian listed earlier.

GETTING IT TOGETHER AND CUTTING AND PASTING

CHAPTER 12

The writing itself, and the
importance of editing and revising

You have researched your topic until you know it inside
and out. You have collected information on cards, in note-
books, or in folders. What now? How do you begin putting it
all together into a cohesive and comprehensible format? Not

everyone is born a great writer. You may be the exception to the rule, and if so, you may choose to skip this chapter. But for many people, putting something on paper for someone else to read and evaluate can be a trying experience. It need not be.

First, gather your information and decide just what you want to say. Then prepare a simple outline covering the major areas within your topic. Put items down in the order in which you want them to appear. This will be a mere skeleton of your paper, to be fleshed out with the data you have collected.

Your paper should have an introduction. This tells the reader why you chose the topic, how you researched it, and what you hope to explain.

Similarly, the conclusion of the paper should briefly cover the major points you have made and state your findings.

Once your outline is completed, arrange your information according to the various headings and subheadings of the outline. Following your outline, begin at the beginning, piecing in all the information where it belongs. For this first draft, you need not worry immediately about how well it reads. Just get the facts down in reasonable order.

If you are typing, double or triple space to leave room between the lines for additional information or changes. If you are writing in longhand, skip every other line.

Now, read it over. You will probably note that it makes abrupt statements without what are called "transitional phrases." These are the key to a steady, unbroken flow of readable information.

For example:

In 1973 there was a recession. In 1973 the college student population rose. In 1973 there was high unemployment. In 1973 car sales were down. The relief rolls rose in 1973.

All the information is there, but the structure is choppy. Compare it with this:

> *During* the 1973 recession, there was high unemployment, the relief rolls rose, *and* college student enrollments increased. *In addition,* car sales were down.

It does not take much to make the sentences and phrases flow smoothly. Another technique is to use synonyms. When reading through your first draft, watch for the same words appearing over and over. Try to eliminate them or find synonyms for them. For example:

> Many authors have written about the Great Depression, and different authors have different opinions about the Great Depression's causes. Nevertheless, most authors agree that many people suffered economic hardship during the Great Depression. In some ways, the effects of the Great Depression are still with us.

These sentences can be rewritten to read more smoothly:

> Numerous books have been written about the Great Depression, and opinions vary as to its causes. Nevertheless, most authors agree that many people suffered economic hardship during the 1930s. In some ways, the effects of that crisis remain.

One key to good writing is keeping it free of unnecessary jargon. Almost all disciplines today have their own "language" that the "in" people understand. You have, undoubtedly, come across some of that in your research. You may find an article or book you think is important to your interpretation of the topic, but you cannot understand it after wading through pages of unintelligible jargon. This is something to avoid in your own work. You want your paper to be understood by your professor as well as the other students. By all means, use those economics terms you understand, but avoid those which do nothing to improve the quality of your term paper.

Keep the language simple and straightforward. Say exactly what you mean. If you write something and follow it with "in other words," you should have explained it more clearly the first time. Phrases such as "in the event that" can be reduced to "if"; "at this point in time" means "now" or "presently." Search for wordy phrases that can be reduced to one or two concise words. You would be surprised at how many, such as those above, are employed merely to fill space.

Sentence structure is a serious problem for many students. You may have all the information you need and thoroughly understand the subject, but you may not be able to construct a sentence correctly. Without this ability, the information you have to impart may be lost to your reader. Remember that a sentence consists of two major parts, the subject and the predicate. The subject is a noun with modifiers and is the topic of a sentence. The predicate consists of the verb or action word and the other information that tells about the subject. For example: *John stumbled down the stairs*. "John" is the subject, and what he did ("stumbled down the stairs") is the predicate. A slightly more complicated sentence is: *The call for wage-price controls brought about the appointment of a special aide to the President*. The subject is "the call for wage-price controls," and the predicate is the action portion of the sentence, "brought about the appointment of a special aide to the President."

Granted, sentences are usually more involved than these examples, but you should always be able to pinpoint the subject and the predicate without difficulty if the sentence is to be easily understood. If you find you have trouble with this in your writing, you might be using run-on sentences.

These consist of two or more sentences joined in one incomprehensible "sentence." For example:

> *Due to the bumper crop of wheat this year, farmers will be receiving lower rates on the domestic market they hope to sell more overseas.*

This sentence can easily be converted to two clear sentences with the placement of a period after "market." By changing some words, it could be maintained as one sentence. "Due to the bumper crop of wheat this year, farmers will be receiving lower rates on the domestic market and are hoping to sell more overseas." Also, a semicolon might be placed after "market" because the two subjects are so closely related.

A run-on sentence should not be confused with a compound sentence, one in which two or more subject-predicate parts can be joined by commas or semicolons:

> *I am researching the paper, Susan is writing it, and Pat is editing it.*
> *Car sales are increasing; this could result in higher employment.*

Look for run-on sentences when reading through your first draft. Use punctuation or rewording to create a better sentence structure.

Another common writing problem, which probably stems from incorrect use of spoken English, involves singular and plural pronouns.

> *Everyone thinks they should have a substantial wage increase.*

"Everyone" (note the *one*) "thinks" (singular form of the verb) "they" (plural pronoun referring incorrectly to a singular subject) "should have a" (singular) "substantial wage increase." The plural pronoun "they" is referring to the singular subject, "everyone." Instead of they, he or she could be used to bring the pronoun into harmony with the subject. Or the sentence could be changed to read: "People think they should have a substantial wage increase."

Another writing problem is unclear pronoun references.

The President said he would see the lawmaker after he called him.

This sentence could mean:

The President said he would first call the lawmaker, then see him.

It also could mean:

After the lawmaker called, the President said he would see him.

These are only a few of the mistakes commonly found in college term papers. This book is not intended as a grammar text, but there are several excellent reference works for both grammar and style available in libraries and bookstores:

The Elements of Style, by William Strunk, Jr., and E. B. White (New York: Macmillan Co., 1972).

The College Writers Handbook, by Suzanne Jacobs and Roderick Jacobs (New York: John Wiley & Sons, Inc., 1976).

Student's Guide for Writing College Papers, by Kate L. Turabian (Chicago: University of Chicago Press, 1976).

Many people have written a paper the night before it was due. The first draft is the final draft, and the professor can spot it instantly. There are misspelled words, run-on sentences, incomplete phrases, missing lines. There is no doubt that this has been the downfall of what might otherwise have been excellent papers.

Editing is a necessary process in the preparation of term papers. After your first draft is completed, if you have the luxury of time, leave the paper for a while and do something else. When you return to it later, you should be able to reread it more objectively. With pencil in hand and scissors nearby, begin reading. Proofread for errors in spelling, punctuation, verb tense, and so forth. If you are unsure about the spelling or definition of a word, dictionaries have been known to be of help in these situations. If you require another word with the same meaning as the one you have used, try checking a thesaurus. Make sure that the items in your paper appear in the most logical sequence. If you find a sentence or paragraph out of place, grab your scissors, cut it out, and paste or tape it to the correct spot. Write any additional information in the double-spaced lines of your first draft.

Look over your footnotes. Are they numbered correctly, and do the numbers refer to the correct items? Are authors' names spelled correctly? Is the form the correct one?

Does the bibliography list all your reference materials? Are they in alphabetical order by author? Have you supplied all the necessary information for each title?

Finally, does what you have written make sense? Could some thoughts be stated in a more concise manner? Do you have too many thoughts jumbled into one enormous sentence or into a run-on sentence? Try to break these down to give the reader some help in understanding your points.

When you have satisfied yourself on these items, type your final draft, double spaced. Unless you have been given permission to do otherwise, the paper must be typed, either by you or a typist. When you complete each page, proofread it. If you have left out a crucial paragraph, proofing as you go along will save you the trouble of retyping all the pages that follow the mistake.

If your professor has special quirks, such as insisting on subheadings within the paper, specific margins, and the like, be sure to follow these guidelines.

That's all there is to it. Good luck!

Part II

The Best Papers from the M.S.U. Economist

LOG EXPORT RESTRICTIONS

By Richard Craswell

Traditionally, international economists have aimed their criticisms at measures to protect domestic industries by restricting *imports* of foreign goods; exports have always had the support of everyone. More recently, however, the rising costs of lumber products, in general, and of housing, in particular, have created political demands for a cutback on the exportation of logs to Japan. The issue has received little attention in the Midwest, but the Senate Banking, Housing and Urban Affairs Committee has held hearings in San Francisco, California, and Portland, Oregon, and a bill has been introduced in the Senate that would eventually shut off log exports completely. The most recent estimates indicate that the bill will probably pass.

Although the measure seems to differ from standard protectionist proposals, it is still an attempt to "protect" domestic sales by restricting free trade, and it can be analyzed using many of the same theoretical tools. That is the aim of this paper. Before I consider the export restriction proposals, a brief overview of the industry will be a helpful introduction.

The western softwoods industry is centered in the coastward halves of Oregon and Washington and extends into northern California and coastal Alaska. The primary wood is Douglas fir, followed by western hemlock and various true firs, cedars, and pines.

About 58 percent of this wood grows on federal lands, the rest being found on private holdings of various sizes. The logged timber is processed, usually in local mills (although exports to Japan have been almost entirely raw logs), and used for a number of wood products; housing and construction are by far the largest users. Smaller logs are cut into "chips" and used for pulp in the paper and paper products industries.

Because of its dependence on the housing industry (which itself is highly sensitive to changes in the interest rate), the lumber business is subject to sharp fluctuations, and therein lies part of the problem. From a downturn in 1968 and 1969, the housing boom of the 1970s sparked sharp increases in lumber prices, and these are continuing. As of February 1973, wholesale lumber prices were 50 percent and more above 1972 prices,[1] with some areas reporting increases of up to 30 percent per month. A dealer in the San Francisco area reported: "They're asking us when it's going to stop, and we don't have an answer for them. Lumber prices are a week-to-week proposition now."[2]

Given the situation, it is hardly surprising that exports to Japan have come under attack. Japan's housing boom began around 1963, and exports have continued to rise since then. Total softwood log exports from the coastal states were at 350 million board feet (m.b.f.) in 1962, more than doubled (750 m.b.f.) the following year, and rose steadily to 3 billion board feet in 1972; figures for the early months of 1973 show a further increase.[3] The factions have formed along predictable lines, with mill operators and builders urging an embargo on exports, while logging companies, port officials, and longshoremen defend the exports. The arguments have ranged from reasoned to emotional. One Oregon milltown newspaper warned: "Unless we're careful, our children may find 'made in Japan' stamped on the plywood and wall paneling they'll be needing to build their homes when they grow up."[4]

This paper is an attempt to discuss the economic facts. I shall begin by analyzing the restriction proposal using the standard two-country static equilibrium model. I shall then expand the analysis by relaxing each of these limiting assumptions in turn.

The Two-Country Static Equilibrium Model

Suppose that the only two countries involved in the lumber trade were the United States and Japan, that the industry had reached an equilibrium, and that demand and supply conditions were relatively stable. In that case, the log trade could be represented by means of the graph in Figure 1: DD, FD, and TD represent the domestic demand, foreign demand, and total demand (the sum of the two), while S indicates the domestic supply of lumber. With no restrictions on exports, the equilibrium price would be P_1, with FQ_1, DQ_1, and TQ_1 representing (respectively) the quantities bought by foreigners and by domestic purchasers, and the total quantity produced and sold.

With an embargo on log exports, however, foreign demand would cease. (I am assuming a total embargo; the effects would be the same but smaller in degree under quotas or partial restrictions.) In this case, the only relevant curves become the supply and domestic demand curves (S and DD), with $DQ_2 = TQ_2$ being the quantity sold to domestic purchasers at a price of P_2 at equilibrium.

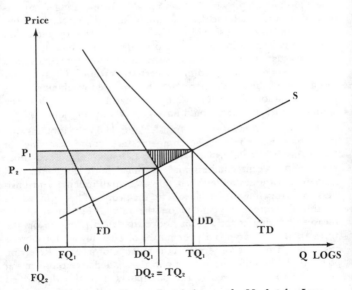

Figure 1. *Effects of an Export Restriction on the Market for Logs*

Note: The foreign demand is shown somewhat larger here than it actually is in order better to illustrate the effect. In 1972, exports amounted to approximately one-seventeenth of domestic sales.

It will be seen at once that this represents an increase in supply to domestic lumber purchasers at a lower price, an obvious gain to the sawmills. The fully shaded trapezoid is essentially a measure of this gain: the decrease in price per log (P_2 minus P_1) times the number of logs purchased (from DQ_1 to DQ_2). But it must be noted that what the log purchasers gain, the log suppliers lose; the reduction in price constitutes a direct transfer from the logging companies to the mills. The loggers are selling no more logs at this price (in fact, the total quantity sold has decreased from TQ_1 to TQ_2); the reduction is just that much less that must be paid by millowner to logger each time a log changes hands. What the mills gain, the logging companies lose.[5]

There is some controversy over whether this reduction in cost to the sawmills would be passed on to builders and eventually to the consumer. The question is whether the mills could significantly increase production, or whether they are already operating at capacity, and thus the inelastic demand would keep the price of lumber up. Senator Alan Cranston of California believes that the reduction would be passed on in the form of price decreases,[6] but an official of the Western Wood Products Association (which represents mills and woodworkers) admitted in a speech in Portland, Oregon, that "even if all of the 1972 exports, which amounted to about six percent of domestic softwood consumption, had been available to the domestic market, prices would have been about the same."[7]

One still could favor such a transfer, purely on the grounds that millworkers and construction companies are "more deserving" or "more needy" than loggers and longshoremen, if for no other reason. (At recent congressional hearings, both sides presented numerous witnesses telling their tale of a small independent businessman struggling to provide jobs for the people of his town, whose continued existence depended on the success or defeat of the measure limiting exports.) But notice that even if one favors the transfer, the embargo is a poor means of effecting it, for more is taken away from the loggers than the mill operators gain. Referring to Figure 1, the suppliers lose not only the shaded area representing that which is transferred to the purchasers, but also the striped area.

This triangle of deadweight loss corresponds to the decrease in business that was formerly exported but which has not been absorbed by the domestic market. More specifically, it represents such woods as Port Orford cedar, popular in Japan but with only a weak market in this country, and other logs which are not profitable to cut and transport at domestic prices. There are indications that this type of wood is a significant part of total exports. Miner H. Baker, vice-president and chief economist, First National Bank of Seattle, reported: "If you look at the breakdown of export between Douglas-fir and hemlock and other species, it is vastly different from the mix of forest products in the domestic market. This does not mean that there is not some Douglas-fir going to export, or that in some cases the hemlock exported would not have been purchased for domestic use. But on balance it is a different mix."[8] Richard Woods, president, Western Farm Forestry Association, put it more bluntly: "Until the Japanese came along, hemlock logs mostly went into chips."[9] Thus, while an embargo would accomplish the transfer from log suppliers to log purchasers, it would do so only by costing the loggers much more than the millers would gain. For those who still favor such a redistribution, a program of taxing logging companies and port workers and giving the proceeds to mills and lumber products dealers would be a more efficient solution; in no case would the embargo be the preferred policy.

This consideration alone would argue against the policy of log export limitations, but more important are the dynamic aspects ruled out by the above model. The assumptions of a two-country market, static supply and demand conditions, and a market in equilibrium are all unrealistic in some degree, and I shall now relax each of them. In each case, the effect is to make export restrictions even less desirable as an economic policy.

Relaxing the Assumptions

The most obvious oversimplification is contained in the two-country assumption. Clearly, there are more countries involved in the lumber trade than the exporting United States and the importing Japan. In fact, when all lumber products are considered together, the United States is actually an *importer,* with net imports in 1972 of 4.1 billion board feet and total imports of 7.6 b.b.f. (virtually all from Canada). This introduces a new factor into the analysis. With Japanese demand at its current level, a reduction of the logs available from the United States would force Japan to turn elsewhere. Canada is currently Japan's leading foreign supplier of lumber, and a study conducted by the Boston Consulting Group for the 1972 Senate hearings predicted that the effect of log export restrictions would be to triple the quantity of logs purchased by Japan from Canada within five years.[10]

The effect, of course, would be to reduce the amount of lumber available to the U.S. market. In effect, U.S. purchasers would still be bidding against the Japanese. In the model used above, this situation can best be represented by a reduction (leftward shift) in the supply curve, with the result that the price and quantity of logs available for domestic use may not change that significantly. Figure 2 illustrates this shift. While the benefits to lumber purchasers would be decreased, the loss of revenue to domestic log suppliers would be as high as before. The chief effect would be to transfer to Canadian logging companies the U.S. share of the lucrative Japanese market, while the quantity of logs available domestically would increase only slightly if at all.

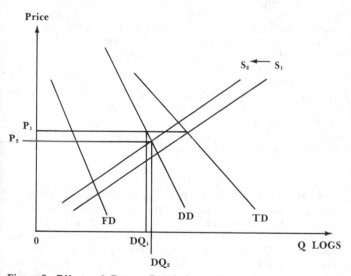

Figure 2. *Effects of Export Restrictions, Taking into Account the Canadian Market*

Note: S_1 and S_2 now represent the total supply of logs (U.S. and Canadian) available to the U.S. domestic market before and after the restrictions, respectively.

The inclusion of other countries in the model has reduced further the attractiveness of a restriction on exports, but the case does not end here. The model also assumes a static market, with stable supply and demand curves. However, if there is one characteristic of the lumber market today, it is the fact that it is *not* static. Two dynamic factors make the case against export restrictions even stronger.

First, a general dynamic gain from free trade is particularly applicable here. The international market, by virtue of its larger size, will reduce the effects of local fluctuations and result in a more stable industry. As was noted earlier, the lumber market has been marked by extreme fluctuations, most of these traceable to unstable demand for housing, which depends heavily (through mortgages) on the prevailing interest rates. But an international market overcomes the fluctuations caused by varying national monetary policies and housing programs to make for a more stable market. This not only reduces the likelihood of severe depressions in the industry, but also is important for planning in an industry in which long-range decisions must be made because of the time lag of forest management and reforestation programs. George Weyerhauser, president, Weyerhauser, Inc. (the largest holder of private timberland in the United States), made this point in a recent interview: "Foreign markets don't follow the same cycles as ours. That smooths out your business curves and allows the forester to manage his lands better. That's the key to the future."[11]

Second (and perhaps more important), the present state of the industry, that is, rapidly rising demand, makes the export market important because of its incentive to use forest lands more productively. The Director of Economics and Marketing, U.S. Forest Service, said before a Senate committee last year: "Timber supply with present management would not be sufficient beyond the next ten years or so to meet rising demands [at current prices]. Therefore, we either have to have higher prices in the longer run to make supply and demand come into balance, or else we have to take other steps such as intensifying management to improve the supply situation."[12] And it is just this intensive management which the export market has stimulated. W. Lee Robinson of the Longview Fibre Company has said: "Remembering back to the early 1960's, the export market created a meaningful stimulus for more intensive management of lands owned by the company. The market for 'Jap piling' stimulated commercial thinnings which enhanced the quality and quantity of better grade sawlogs and peelable material left in the company's forest for continued growth and harvesting in later years."[13] The vice-president of a larger company, Weyerhauser, echoed this conclusion: "Washington's export trade thus has been generated not through expansion of harvest acres or decline in domestic industry, but through increasing the yield from the acres harvested . . . . In other words, export markets have been a net addition to Washington's economy."[14] When the dynamic factors are considered, the log export trade may well be of some benefit even to the building industry and other purchasers of lumber, since a stable market and increased yield can only help these interests in the long run.

Finally, the last assumption to relax is that of a market in equilibrium. Normally, this is a valid assumption to make (in the long run, a free market will tend to equalize supply and demand), but the imposition of price ceilings in August 1971 removed its validity. Lumber companies did develop a number of ingenious ways of avoiding the controls,[15] but prices were still held down by phases I and II, and although phase III officially relies on "voluntary restraint," logging and lumber operators are still cautious. *Crow's Forest Products Digest,* an industry marketing journal, reported the change as follows: "Effects on the market were not fully apparent as this was written. Most forest products companies were being very cautious pending examination of the fine print . . . . Government officials kept referring to the 'club in the closet,' meaning that the CLC can apply controls selectively at any time."[16] More recently, a Western Wood Products Association official estimated that there was still a 50-50 chance that lumber would be back under phase II types of controls in the near future.[17]

In this sort of environment, whether the controls were open or implied made little difference; they still had the predictable effect of holding down supply in the face of rising demand. *Business Week* cites examples of mills that closed operations when the Price Commission's profit limits had been reached for that year. It concluded: "Lumber production is at record levels, but it is apparently being held below its potential by producers that do not want to violate the Price Commission's profit-margin limitations."[18] The *Wall Street Journal* reported the same thing, noting that although "the idea that controls may have inhibited the growth in lumber supplies is a touchy issue within the Nixon administration," the Assistant Secretary of the Treasury for Economic Affairs conceded that controls were restricting lumber production.[19]

I will not argue here whether the controls were politically necessary or whether they should even be continued. But as long as they remain in effect, the export market takes on crucial importance as the only market encouraging lumber producers to increase supply to meet demand. The examples cited earlier of exports increasing domestic yield are pertinent here; a more striking effect can be seen by comparing the lumber situation with that in the pulp and paper products industry. The two (for obvious reasons) face similar supply conditions, but there is virtually no export market for Northwest wood pulp products. All sales are made in the controlled domestic market. Although the demand for pulp and paper is expected to rise significantly over the next few years, the industry is doing virtually nothing to increase output. In fact, industry sources recently predicted that because of the controls (as well as pressures from environmentalists) the growth of capital assets over the next three years would be the industry's smallest since World War II.[20]

There are a number of other issues bearing on the log export matter which, because of space limitations, I must omit. A full discussion of the lumber industry would include federal forestry practices (as noted, these affect 58 percent of the softwood sawlog inventory), which have been criticized by both loggers and mill operators as contributing to the scarcity. Environmentalists have added their support to the embargo, and I have not discussed their position, although it does not change the basic issues. Regardless of the level accepted as the optimal balance between timberlands used for recreation and for lumber production, all the above arguments still hold. I have also set aside the effect on the balance of trade as a whole. (A consideration of this effect would argue against the embargo. In 1972, log exports to Japan decreased the U.S. deficit by $634 million.[21]) The same is true of our political relations with Japan, which have hardly been helped by administration efforts to reduce log exports, especially in view of our sharp criticism of Japan for not importing enough U.S. goods in other areas.

However, these other considerations do not weaken the case for log exports, and the issues dealt with in depth are sufficient to establish the case. Even in a stable market, export restrictions would help the sawmills and builders only by hurting loggers, and it is doubtful whether any of the gains would be passed on to consumers. Furthermore, the cost to the suppliers exceeds any gain to the purchasers, and when the shift of Japanese business to Canada is noted, the gains to the mill operators tend to diminish, while the loggers are as bad off as before. Dynamic considerations of increased yield and a stable market make an embargo even less desirable, and as long as price or profit controls remain in effect, the export market becomes even more beneficial. In sum, even in an equilibrium economy, log exports are important. When all factors are considered, it is not an exaggeration to say they are crucial.

Does this mean that log exports will not be restricted? Of course not. The Morse amendment already restricts the export of logs cut from federally owned land, and the administration recently announced the success of its efforts to persuade the Japanese "voluntarily" to cut back their purchases of logs from the West Coast in 1974 to approximately 90 percent of 1972 levels.[22] Politically, buyers of lumber outnumber the sellers at the polls, and although the demand for housing may be starting to level off, lumber prices are still rising. In a country in which the political climate demands that politicians "do something," regardless of the effects, I will not attempt to predict the results. In the event that complete export restrictions are imposed, all the economist can do is echo Bastiat:

> Good Lord! What a lot of trouble to prove in political economy that two and two make four; and if you succeed in doing so, people cry, 'It is so clear that it is boring.' Then they vote as if you had never proved anything at all.

Notes

1. From a report by United Press International, March 28, 1973.
2. Ray Ryan, manager, J. E. Higgins Lumber Company. Reported in the *San Francisco Examiner,* March 25, 1973.
3. U.S. Department of Commerce figures for the years up to 1972 are from *Log Export Controls,* Hearings before the Subcommittee on International Finance of the Senate Committee on Banking, Housing, and Urban Affairs, 92nd Cong., 2d sess., June 8, 9, and 12, 1972, p. 153. The 1973 figures are from a U.S. Forest Service release, carried by the *Seattle Times,* April 15, 1973, p. A5. All further trade figures will be from the U.S. Department of Commerce unless otherwise noted.

4. From an editorial in the *Springfield* [Ore.] *News,* March 13, 1972. Reprinted in U.S. Senate, *Log Export Controls,* p. 52.
5. The bifurcation of the industry into loggers and millers is, of course, an oversimplification. The factions are not split precisely along those lines, and many sawmills own their own stands of timber and thus could be included in both groups. Economically, however, this separation by function is valid, and the basic principles expressed here still hold.
6. Reported by the *Seattle Times,* April 14, 1973, p. 816.
7. H. A. Roberts, executive vice-president, in the *San Francisco Chronicle,* May 3, 1973, p. 35.
8. U.S. Senate, *Log Export Controls,* p. 39.
9. From the *Seattle Times,* April 12, 1973, p. D3.
10. U.S. Senate, *Log Export Controls,* pp. 408–409. It should be pointed out that while some provinces (such as British Columbia) allow the export only of "finished lumber products," this has had little effect. What are exported are "cants," or logs with the bark peeled off and the sides roughly squared. This "finishing" is done solely to get around the restrictions; little actual labor is involved, and the cants are treated as ordinary logs would be.
11. *Forbes,* May 15, 1973, p. 86.
12. U.S. Senate, *Log Export Controls,* p. 275.
13. Ibid., p. 207.
14. Ibid., pp. 102–103.
15. See the *Wall Street Journal,* September 29, 1972, p. 1. Ironically, the story also notes that the controls themselves were encouraging companies to sell their logs in the (uncontrolled) export market.
16. *Crow's Forest Products Digest,* February 1973, p. 9.
17. H. A. Roberts, executive vice-president, in the *San Francisco Chronicle,* May 3, 1973, p. 35.
18. *Business Week,* November 25, 1972, p. 24.
19. *Wall Street Journal,* November 21, 1972, p. 3.
20. From the *Wall Street Journal,* October 26, 1972, p. 20.
21. Figures of the Japanese Ministry of International Trade and Industry (MITI), carried in a United Press International release, May 15, 1973.
22. *Seattle Times,* April 10, 1973, p. C16.

Bibliography

"The Administration's Big Stick." *Forbes,* May 15, 1973, p. 86.

"The General Outlook." *Crow's Forest Products Digest,* February 1973, p. 9.

Guthrie, John A., and George R. Armstrong. *Western Forest Industry: An Economic Outlook.* Baltimore: Johns Hopkins Press, 1961.

Lindley, H. Clark, Jr. "Lumbering Alone." *Wall Street Journal,* January 2, 1973, p. 20.

Log Export Controls. Hearings before the Subcommittee on International Finance, Senate Committee on Banking, Housing, and Urban Affairs. Washington, D.C.: U.S. Government Printing Office, 1972. GPO catalog No. Y4.822/3:L82.

"Lumber Companies Violating Price Controls soon Will Be Penalized, Commission Warns." *Wall Street Journal,* November 21, 1972, p. 3.

"Lumber Prices Jump as Demand for Boards Soars." *Wall Street Journal,* September 29, 1972, p. 1.

"Pulp, Paper Concerns Plan only Small Rise in Output." *Wall Street Journal,* October 26, 1972, p. 20.

San Francisco Chronicle, San Francisco Examiner, and *Seattle Times,* various issues, March through May 1973.

"What Keeps Lumber Prices High?" *Business Week,* November 25, 1972, pp. 24–25.

This paper was written for a course in international trade and finance. Richard Craswell majored in political science and economics and is now an attorney at the Federal Trade Commission.

THE ECONOMIC EFFECTS OF BILLBOARD CONTROL

By Brant Freer and Ronald Sutton

> I think that I shall never see
> A billboard lovely as a tree
> And unless the billboards fall
> I'll never see a tree at all.
> — Ogden Nash

How has billboard regulation affected Michigan's economy? Before answering this question, we will examine the origins of billboard advertising, recent legislation, and the historical arguments concerning billboard regulation. We then will present evidence dealing with Michigan's billboard legislation and interpret these data.

A major research problem was finding sufficient statistical evidence. As we conducted interviews in both government and advertising agencies, researched library materials, and sifted through public records, it was astonishing how little concrete information there was pertaining to billboards in Michigan. Therefore, we have used studies conducted in other states to help us draw inferences about Michigan.

Origins

The word *advertising* is derived from two Latin words, *ad* ("toward") and *vertere* ("to turn"). The objective of advertising is to turn the attention of a given market of buyers toward a product, service, idea, or personality.[1]

Merchants in Babylonia, considered to be the birthplace of outdoor advertising, were among the first to realize the value of hanging signs above their places of business to identify their trades. It was in the Roman Empire, however, that the practice became widespread. Since few people could read or write, objects and animals were used to inform travelers.

Signs became so important to merchants and innkeepers throughout Europe that, during the fourteenth century, official edicts required their use to identify all businesses properly. The sign became, in actuality, a license to do business. In Paris and London, coach painters began painting the signs, and by the 1800s the streets became virtual art galleries.

On May 9, 1862, at Longsight, the first meeting of the United Kingdom Billposters' Association was held. These billposters proclaimed in an early flyer:

> The power of the press is great in spreading the news, but the power of the placard is equally great, insofar that many who read their papers regularly never look at the advertisements. We place them conspicuously before their eyes, so that they cannot avoid seeing them upon every wall compelling them to read whether they will or no.[2]

Billboards in the United States

The first recorded leasings of billboards occurred in the United States in 1867. P. T. Barnum, the famous circus entrepreneur, became the biggest user of outdoor advertising in the country. Traveling circuses and salesmen, along with the merchants, were the main users of the medium.

In 1872 the International Bill Posters' Association of North America was formed at St. Louis, Missouri. Although it proved to be a rather useless organization, it did lead to the formation of state associations, with Michigan leading the way in 1875. In the early years, these associations worked mainly for the standardization of poster sizes. However, when burlesque shows began to spread "offense paper," the associations refused to handle the advertisements, the earliest recorded censorship exercised by an advertising medium over any material.

The development of the automobile brought a boom to the billboard industry far beyond anything imaginable at the time. America became a nation on the move, and billboards became a major means of communication from merchants to consumers.

By 1955 there was, as Clifton Enfield states, "a steadily growing demand for the regulation of outdoor advertising adjacent to the nation's highways."[3] The first step toward this goal was the Federal Highway Act of 1956. Although the act contained no provisions for controlling advertising, it gave an impetus to those who believed such control was needed. The Federal-Aid Highway Act of 1958 was the first legislation to regulate outdoor advertising. In general, the act applied to the portions of the interstate systems constructed upon completely new right-of-way, outside commercial or industrial areas. National standards were provided for

   (1) official signs;

   (2) signs advertising the sale or lease of property upon which they were located;

   (3) signs advertising activities within twelve miles of those signs; and

   (4) signs authorized by state law, giving information in the specific interest of the public.[4]

President Lyndon Johnson was not satisfied with these controls, and in 1965 he recommended new legislation. The result was the Highway Beautification Act of 1965, which is most important to this study.

Highway Beautification Act of 1965

Passed by Congress on September 22, 1965, the Highway Beautification Act contained one important section dealing with the control of outdoor advertising. Such control was necessary, in the opinion of the Congress, in order to "protect the public investment in highways, to promote the safety and recreational values of public travel, and to preserve natural beauty."[5]

Any state that did not enact "effective control" by January 1, 1968, would have its federal highway aid cut by 10 percent until such control was enacted. The money withheld would be reapportioned to other states.

What was this "effective control"? States were to pass legislation which prohibited outdoor advertising within 660 feet of the edge of a highway except for

(1) official signs and notices (for example, gas — food — lodging) and those signs legally erected;

(2) advertisements for the sale of property upon which they are located; and

(3) advertisements designating activities conducted on the property on which such activities are located.

The legally erected signs mentioned in item (1) above are those constructed and maintained within 660 feet of the highway on lands that are either zoned industrial or commercial or unzoned areas designated as primary industrial or commercial by agreement between the states and the Secretary of Commerce.[6]

This act differs from the 1958 law in that it provides a greater incentive for states to enact legislation governing advertising. The penalty for noncompliance in 1965 was a 10 percent cut in aid, whereas a one percent bonus for compliance had been offered in 1958.

Michigan Highway Advertising Act of 1972
(P.A. 106)

Following passage of the Highway Beautification Act, Michigan had no choice but to pass a law of its own. The first effort, in 1966, was weak and very ineffective. Billboard advertising in Michigan continued to grow virtually unchecked. In 1972 Michigan enacted the Highway Advertising Act. Its objectives were stated in Section 3:

> To improve and enhance scenic beauty consistent with the provision of Section 131 of Title 23 of the U.S. Code, as amended, the legislature finds it appropriate to regulate and control outdoor advertising adjacent to the interstate highway, freeway and primary highway systems within this state and that outdoor advertising is a legitimate commercial use of private property, is an integral part of the marketing function and an established segment of the economy of this state.[7]

The act covers essentially the same area as the federal law concerning which signs may be legally constructed along interstate highways. Other important features include the following:

(1) anyone wishing to erect a billboard along an interstate or primary highway must obtain a permit from the Michigan Department of Highways;

(2) if the department removes any sign that was lawful before the 1972 act, it must pay a "just" compensation to the owner of that billboard; and

(3) penalties for violating this act are fines not less than $100.00 nor more than $1,000.00.

An important point is that the legislature believed it had little choice in the matter. Noncompliance meant a 10 percent loss of federal highway appropriations — millions of dollars annually — and the legislators felt that the state could not afford such a loss.

Arguments in Favor of Billboard Control

The main justification for billboard regulation is that billboards detract from the scenic beauty of the surrounding countryside. This view was expressed by Senator Maurine Neuberger of Oregon: "My concern is that these thoroughfares are running between corridors of garish and unsightly billboards, rather than vistas of scenic countryside."[8]

Americans have long been proud of their environmental heritage, but in the past few years many people have become fearful as to its future. Pollution and ecology have become household words. Over the past decade, many laws have been enacted in response to pressure from interest groups, such as the Sierra Club and the National Wildlife Federation, and the general public. Much of this legislation followed from the Highway Beautification Act of 1965.

Since one of the easiest targets was the visual "pollution" caused by billboards, legislators chose this as an early area of concentration. When asked to defend their actions with respect to the environment and ecology, congressmen could point with pride to their vote for the bill, probably one of the major reasons it was passed at that time.

Arguments against Billboard Control

One of the main objections to controlling billboards is that the general public apparently favors their continued use. This feeling has been voiced repeatedly in various polls. For example, on July 7, 1965, soon after Lyndon Johnson placed the highway beautification bill before Congress, the Gallup Organization asked a representative national cross section of the public: "What are the things you would do if it were your job to beautify America?" Their answers are given below.[9]

	Percent
Clean up highways, stop littering	30
Clear slums, renovate or replace old buildings	23
Beautify the highways, plant trees and flowers	19
Eliminate junkyards	19
Eliminate billboards	17
Improve and increase parks, campsites	14
Encourage everyone to clean up his own property	13
Eliminate water pollution	4
Eliminate air pollution	1
Miscellaneous	4
Satisfied now, "Looks all right to me"	2
Don't know	1

An even more surprising result occurred from a 1964 poll taken by the Garden Clubs of Virginia, a group vigorously in favor of billboard control. In cooperation with the State Department of Highways, volunteers stopped 5,997 drivers and asked them a series of questions to gauge their feelings about billboards. The final question was: "Do you have *any* objection to billboards?" This obviously was intended to elicit many responses against outdoor advertising, but 70 percent of the drivers said they had *no objections.*[10]

It appears that consumers want freedom of choice in their purchases along highways, and that without billboards they feel that their freedom is impaired. "To rely on the 'Gas — Food — Lodging' announcement is to participate in a lottery. That is particularly so along the increasing number of superhighways which themselves restrict one's ability to search out the goods and services of his choice."[11]

The second major criticism of the control of outdoor advertising is that the "scenic" areas the laws are designed to protect are not really very scenic. A stretch of prairie, miles of barren wasteland, or grainfields are often more boring than scenic to many travelers. In fact, some would argue that billboards actually break the monotony on freeways and in so doing reduce the accident rate. A 1955 study by the Michigan State Highway Department, in cooperation with the U.S. Bureau of Public Roads, came to the following conclusion: "The laboratory results showed that numerous signs in the driver's field of vision in no way influenced efficiency at the wheel adversely, and in fact seemed slightly beneficial. The difference was about 10 percent in favor of conditions with signs."[12]

The third major fault of the controls is their expense in terms of lost business and lost firms. Some consider it a paradox to spend money encouraging tourism and travel, while at the same time prohibiting advertising which would promote that end. "If the Michigan Highway Department's edict is enforced and business establishments have no way to direct tourists off the main highway, then the department will have effectively removed about 25 percent of available cabins and resorts in the Upper Peninsula," said Ken Dorman, president of the Upper Michigan Tourist Association.[13] Elmer Warner, president of the Michigan Motel and Resort Association, gave the following testimony in 1965 during the federal hearings on the law:

> Due to the fact that nearly 100 percent of the motels and resorts of Michigan are off the freeway system, it is imperative that we have the privilege of letting our motoring public know where we are and what we have to offer in the way of services. This bill would deprive us of this privilege.[14]

Another fault is that rural areas will be forced to bear an inequitable burden in the removal of the signs. Almost all off-premise signs in cities are already in commercial or industrial zones, while almost all the signs in the country are not in such areas. Most of these are not within the 800-foot radius of a commercial activity, as required by Michigan law. In fact, the "1967 Highway Beautification Report" states that of the 889,000 off-premise signs to be condemned, 839,000 (or 94 percent) were condemned because they were not located in the proper areas.[15] These are the advertisements not located in a commercial zone, and they are almost entirely in rural areas.

Major Effects

Decrease in Outdoor Advertising

It is obvious from Table 1 that since 1972 the law has had a substantial effect on the gross number of outdoor signs; in fact,

Table 1. *Billboard Program Status Report, P.A. 106, 1972*

District	1	2	3	4	5	6	7	8	9	Total
1972 Inventory	3024	2044	3745	2368	3514	5178	3678	2933	2338	29,722
Existing signs subject to act	844	773	1292	887	1965	1758	2328	2065	1691	13,603
Permits in force	844	751	1214	834	1770	1658	2234	1870	1542	12,717
Sign removal:										
By others	1000	783	2103	1152	1351	1682	1129	1130	1047	11,377
By state R.O.W.[a]	315	504	679	366	482	990	595	440	156	4,527
Sent to R.O.W.	702	479	923	673	1149	1075	1511	1060	144	7,716
Cleared	537		457		385	410	420	341	32	2,582
Permits for new legal signs since 1972	146	97	150	110	191	169	155	295	216	1,539

SOURCE: Thomas Hawley, Michigan Department of Public Utilities.

[a]The R.O.W. is the right-of-way program whereby the state pays the required just compensation for illegal signs already in existence at the time of enactment of the law. Signs removed by others include any signs removed by any parties other than the state.

there has been a greater than 50 percent decrease. This result was unexpected, based on our informal observations prior to the study. There are two reasons for these impressive figures.

First, fewer highways fall under the controls than the public realizes. The designated highways include only interstate and primary thoroughfares. As an example, in Lansing, Michigan, little of the city's transportation system is actually under control. The few roads that are controlled run through districts which are primarily commercial or industrial, and sign control is therefore minimal. In the Lansing metropolitan area two of the busiest highways, Michigan Avenue and East Grand River Avenue, are not controlled at all.

Second, the 1972 figures are somewhat inflated, since many small and insignificant signs were included. According to Thomas Hawley of the Michigan Department of Public Utilities, Burma Shave, vegetable stand, and dilapidated signs are counted the same as major billboards. If many of the signs removed were of this smaller type, then the effect of the law may be overstated.

Nevertheless, the Michigan law has achieved its goal of lowering the number of signs along interstate and primary highways. It is important to note that the cost was not insignificant. For the removal of approximately 7,000 signs, the state of Michigan and the federal government have spent $11,340,156.

Urban versus Rural Advertising Firms

The Michigan law has had an adverse effect on rural as compared to urban agencies. Thomas Cook, manager, Wolverine Advertising Agency, Owosso, Michigan, stated that he has reduced his staff by 20 percent. Cook also said that billboard construction by rural firms has virtually disappeared along the interstate highway system. Contrast this to the fact that White Advertising in Detroit has increased billboard construction since 1972. Although he would not give any statistics, Roger Lister, general manager, told us that although White's rural sign construction has declined, overall construction has shown a positive increase over the last four years.

Urban agencies have an advantage over rural firms because many city highways do not fall under the jurisdictional control of the regulations. Therefore, many agencies switch from interstate to secondary highways without much loss of market. Thomas Hawley says that this is exactly what is happening; agencies are switching from I-75 to roads such as Woodward Avenue. Rural firms cannot shift to other roads because interstates are the only thoroughfares carrying sufficient traffic to make billboards pay.

Effect on the
Michigan Tourist Industry

Since most billboards have been lost in rural areas, the largest economic effect of the controls will be felt there. It makes sense, then, to examine the largest industry which uses billboards in those areas—tourism. We were unable to find information on losses incurred by Michigan businesses dependent on tourism. The Michigan Chamber of Commerce, Michigan Retail Dealers Association, Michigan Merchants Council, and Michigan Tourist Council all agreed that losses were substantial, but none could offer statistical evidence in support.

This lack of Michigan data forced us to turn to other states to find some measure of the extent of losses. One study that seemed particularly conclusive was conducted in Missouri by Dr. Martin Bell and Dr. Richard Wendall, both professors of marketing at Washington University. They estimated a decline of 22 percent in tourist expenditures in the state as a result of lost billboards under a law similar to Michigan's.[17]

These figures cannot be transferred directly, but as Robert Helwig, Northern Michigan Tourist Association, has said, there has been at least a one percent drop in Michigan tourist expenditures. In 1975, according to the Michigan Tourist Council, tourism accounted for $2.2 billion. Thus, a very conservative estimate of lost income would be $22 million, which seems a considerable cost for a state to bear simply to remove billboards along its interstate highways.

Consumer Loss

The final effect of billboard legislation concerns consumers. Travelers rely on road signs to find particular kinds of lodging, restaurants, service stations, and so forth. Travelers are also interested in historic sites and other tourist attractions in Michigan.

Two examples illustrate the problem. Robert Helwig states that every day motorists are bypassing many scenic areas in northern Michigan, such as Tahquamenon Falls, because they are unaware of their location. This is a real loss to consumers. Another example is the Dony Hotel in Clare. According to Thomas Cook, it has lost so many customers that it is on the verge of going out of business. It cannot advertise its existence to the flow of traffic on U.S. 27, and these are the people for whom the hotel exists.

It seems paradoxical to tear down billboards to enhance the scenery when it means that people unknowingly pass some of the nation's most beautiful areas and facilities.

Conclusions

During the course of this study we found two reasons for the passage of federal and state billboard legislation.

(1) Federal legislators passed the Highway Beautification Act because they believed billboards were eyesores and detrimental to ecological beauty.

(2) Michigan passed the Highway Advertising Act because of a

similar concern, but mainly because it did not want to lose 10 percent of its federal highway appropriations.

The central question is: Were the benefits that Michigan gained by passing such regulations greater than the costs incurred by the state as a whole? The main costs, as we see them, are: (1) monetary loss by the tourist industry; (2) the decline of rural advertising agencies; and (3) detrimental effect on the traveler. We believe these costs far exceed the benefits.

It is impossible to estimate (in dollars) the gains made by the removal of billboards in terms of scenic beauty. It is possible to indicate the amount of money the state saved in federal monies by passing this law. In 1974, according to the Michigan Department of Transportation, federal highway appropriations to the state were $141,319,360. If Michigan had not passed its law, it would have lost approximately $14 million. Our previous and very conservative estimate (compared to the Missouri study) was that Michigan tourist businesses alone stand to lose *$22 million* because of billboard regulations!

Thus, the burden falls on a relatively small segment of the economy, specifically, the tourist industry located mainly in rural areas. In our opinion the state did not act in the best interests of the population as a whole. Monetarily, a better method would be to have the state absorb the $14 million loss in highway aid. Of course, this would ignore the ecological issue. A possible solution would be to make all the costs explicit to the public and then hold a referendum. This would indicate whether ecological beauty means enough to the people of Michigan to justify the income loss. If public sentiment does favor billboard removal, then some method would have to be found to assist the businesses hardest hit by the $22 million loss.

It seems unlikely, given the bureaucratic disposition of state government, that the billboard regulations will be changed, at least in the short run. To ease the burden of the tourist industry and to travelers, we believe the state should operate a special radio frequency and in each district establish a station (subsidized by the state) which carries advertisements by local businessmen. This would socialize, to some extent, the monetary losses of businessmen and would cut those losses significantly. It also would aid consumers by allowing them once again to find the specific businesses with which they wish to deal.

In conclusion, the Michigan Highway Act may have fulfilled the goals that the legislators desired, but in doing so it created what appears to be a larger problem.

Notes

1. The material on origins is from John Houck, ed., *Outdoor Advertising: History and Regulation* (Notre Dame: University of Notre Dame Press, 1969).
2. Cyril Sheldon, *A History of Poster Advertising* (London: Chapman and Hall, 1937), p. 8.
3. Houck, ed., *Outdoor Advertising*, p. 149.
4. Ibid., pp. 162–67.
5. House of Representatives Document #1084, Highway Beautification Act of 1965, Section 131, p. 38.
6. Ibid., p. 39.
7. Highway Advertising Act of 1972, Section 3.
8. Senator Neuberger testifying before the U.S. Senate, Subcommittee on Public Works, *Highway Beautification and Scenic Road Program,* 89th Cong., 1st sess., August 11, 1965, p. 122 (hereafter Senate Hearings, *Road Program.*).
9. Hearings before the U.S. House of Representatives, Committee on Public Works, Subcommittee on Roads, 89th Cong., 1st sess., July 22, 1965, p. 150 (hereafter House Hearings).
10. Hearings before the U.S. Senate, Committee on Public Works, *Highway Beautification and Highway Safety Program,* 90th Cong., 1st sess., June 29, 1967, p. 135.
11. House Hearings, p. 146.
12. Senate Hearings, *Road Program,* p. 215.
13. House Hearings, p. 180.
14. Ibid., p. 455.
15. Senate Hearings, *Road Program,* p. 108.

This paper was written for a course in urban economics. Brant Freer, an economics major, graduated from the University of Michigan Law School in 1979 and is now an attorney. Ronald Sutton, who also majored in economics, received the J.D. degree from Wayne State University and practices law in Lansing, Michigan.

MEDICAID AND THE EMERGENCY ROOM

By John S. MacDonald

Many stories are told today about "the long wait" in some busy metropolitan emergency rooms. I have worked for the past 17 months at St. Lawrence Hospital, Lansing, Michigan, in just such an emergency room. I have heard the complaints of patients, on the one hand—long waits, high prices, rushed attention—and those of medical personnel, on the other—high rate of "nonemergency" visits, crowded facilities, and the alleged abuse of Medicaid. The following study has been motivated by this experience, with special attention given to the controversial Medicaid patient in the emergency room.

Medicaid was born in 1965 when Congress amended the Social Security Act. Title 18 (Medicare) financed medical care for the elderly, and Title 19 (Medicaid) aimed to make quality medical care available to those unable to pay for it. The latter represented a "far more revolutionary departure from previous . . . social welfare philosophy in the United States than Medicare," and due to its relevance to the mainstream of life in poor America, Medicaid is a far more interesting factor in its effect on the poor.[1]

Medicaid was initiated in Michigan in October 1966. Utilizing federal, state, and local funds, it assists two main groups. In Group

93

I are those who receive one of the categorical aids (old-age assistance, aid to the blind, aid to the disabled, and aid to dependent children; in Group II are those who require assistance for medical expenses only. Group I receives the most complete medical coverage, and both groups are covered for emergency outpatient treatment. Medicaid does not cover office appointments for routine physical examinations, as I was informed upon calling several doctors' offices, which confirms that the medical services provided are curative rather than preventive.[2]

Medicaid suddenly made quality medical care a possibility to many people who previously could not afford it. This sudden vast demand put pressure on a medical care system which was not prepared, and in many cases not willing, to meet it. This relationship between a rapidly increasing demand and an inadequate supply created a cost-push inflation in the medical care market. Hospital service charges soared, and physicians' fees continued to rise.[3]

Quality medical care for many of the poor became a "possibility" but not a reality because they were still exploited or refused help by many medical suppliers. For example, some medical practitioners have taken advantage of maximum charges allowable under state fee schedules, thus contributing to the cost-push inflation and depleting Medicaid funds. Other doctors, being in command of such an enormous demand, have become selective against Medicaid.[4]

The recent heavy flow of Medicaid patients to the local emergency room is largely due to these economic pressures, especially the shortage of concerned physicians and medical personnel living and working effectively in poverty areas. It is now clear that merely pumping money into the existing system is not enough.[5]

The St. Lawrence Hospital Emergency Room was taken over in 1967 by a group of three physicians who make it their business to provide 24-hour emergency medical service for the Lansing area. Calling themselves the Ingham Emergency Physicians, P. C., they treat a large number of minor as well as emergency cases. Payment is not demanded upon visit (patients are billed through the mail), and the total facility has established a good general reputation in the local area and among the local poverty-stricken community.

There has been a steady climb in emergency room traffic at St. Lawrence in the past ten years, as Figure 1 clearly shows. It has become so heavy in recent summers that an outsider walking

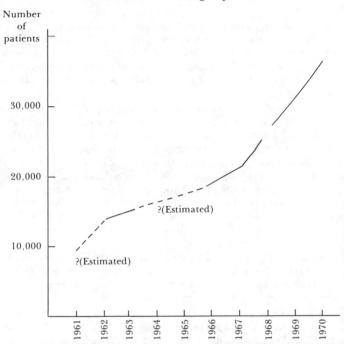

Figure 1. *Patients Seen in Emergency Room of St. Lawrence Hospital,
1961–1971*

SOURCE: Data courtesy of St. Lawrence Emergency Room.

NOTE: Ingham Emergency Physicians, P.C., assumed operations in 1967.

through might wonder if medical care is even possible amid the
chaos and confusion at certain times in the day. Needless to say,
minor cases (such as colds and general aches and pains) at these
times occupy personnel and space needed by those suffering serious
injuries.

It may appear that I am equating all Medicaid patients with
nonemergency visits. This is not my intention, as this would be both
inaccurate and unfair. I am concerned that *the total system* is—although perhaps unintentionally—channeling a large number of the

poor into a facility which is not designed to give total health care, preventive and curative, with follow-up and continuity.

There appears to be an increasing trend of nonemergency type cases at St. Lawrence. The Somers & Somers study of 1967 makes a similar observation: "The vast bulk of the increase in emergency room services does not reflect any significant rise in major trauma or accidents."[6]

Since it is difficult to define a true emergency, there are no data on the exact number of true emergency versus nonemergency cases. Therefore, I have assumed that hospital admissions are roughly proportional to the so-called emergency cases. Figure 2 shows that this component has hardly increased at all since 1969.

Patients covered by Blue Shield medical insurance have been chosen to represent the middle and upper socioeconomic groups in the community (see Figure 2). These persons are more likely to have a family physician and be in the mainstream of the medical care system so that they need not depend so heavily on the emergency room for general medical care.

Recently, the most noticeable change has been in the volume of Medicaid patients. I interpret this rise to be an "overflow" from a medical care system which is not providing the poor with effective service, communication, or education.

Statistics also show an overall increase in Medicaid on the state and local scene since 1968 (see Figure 3). Most evident is the strong effect of the *categorically needy* group on the total (see Figure 4). Further analysis shows that Aid to Dependent Children (ADC) leads this group. The number of ADC cases has skyrocketed since 1967 (see Figure 3), which the state totals reflect. Upon questioning a social worker from the Ingham County Department of Social Services, I learned that the recent trend may be due in part to recent regulations expanding eligibility for ADC. In conclusion, it appears that ADC has set the pace for total Medicaid volume. It is very interesting to note that the rise in emergency room Medicaid volume occurred at roughly the same time the ADC volume was rising.

I recently completed a sample count of 1,000 emergency room patient charts, covering a period from December 1971 through February 1972. Of these, 21 percent were Medicaid patients. This corresponds closely with calculations from the actual emergency room data for the month of January 1972 of 19 percent. In this

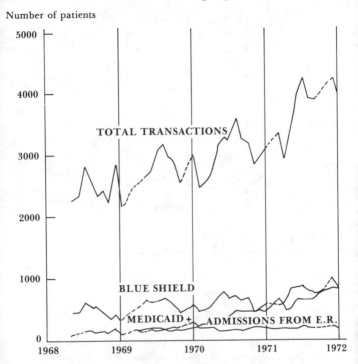

Number of patients

Figure 2. *St. Lawrence Hospital Emergency Room Volume by Components, 1968-1972*

SOURCE: Data Courtesy of Dr. E. C. Nakfoor, St. Lawrence Hospital.

NOTE: This shows three components of the total patient volume at the St. Lawrence Hospital emergency room in the last four years. Notice the rise in Medicaid with respect to admissions and Blue Shield.

representative sample, 82 percent of the Medicaid patients were classified as ADC, and only 49 percent of these ADC cases claimed a private physician. Over half (53 percent) of the ADC patients in the sample were under 18 years of age.

Women and children, especially those living in poverty conditions, have a great need for physicians' services. The incidence of diseases of pregnancy and early childhood and infectious diseases is

Number of cases

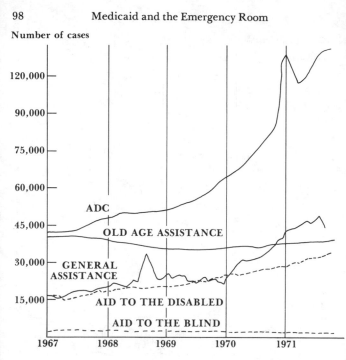

Figure 3. *Public Assistance Money Payments in Michigan, by Case*

SOURCE: Data Courtesy of Michigan Department of Social Services.

NOTE: ADC shows a dramatic climb in recent years, raising the total
volume of Medicaid recipients.

significantly greater in the ghetto. Also, rates of maternal and in-
fant mortality are higher.[7] The need in this group is great, yet they
are streaming into a facility not designed for the delivery of
thorough and *follow-up* medical care.

I interviewed several of the emergency room doctors and social
workers from St. Lawrence Hospital and inquired at the Ingham
County Department of Social Services in search of a deeper understanding of these trends. The shortage of medical physicians,
especially family doctors, was unanimously given as one of the
primary factors in rising emergency room volume. The shortage is
so severe that higher economic classes are affected as well as the

Number of recipients

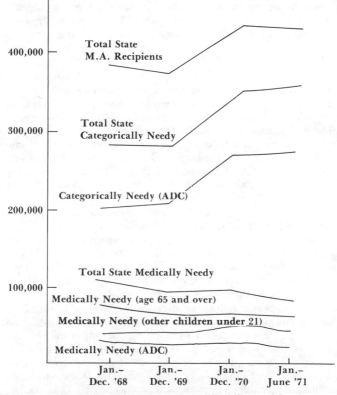

Figure 4. *Medicaid Recipients by Basis of Eligibility and by Type of Case (ADC), 1968–1971*

SOURCE: Data Courtesy of Michigan Department of Social Services.

NOTE: ADC shows a dramatic climb in recent years, raising the total volume of Medicaid recipients.

poor. It is not uncommon to see the financially well-to-do family come to the emergency room for general treatment, explaining that they are new in town and have not been able to find a family doctor, or they are dissatisfied with their present physician and have not found another one.

One important corollary to the physician shortage was added by one of the social workers — the shortage of black doctors. Presently, only one middle-aged general practitioner (G.P.) among the few black M.D.'s in the area is serving a great portion of the black ghetto.

One of the emergency room physicians, a new "fourth man" in the group, shared some interesting comparisons of Lansing to Boston, Massachusetts, from where he commutes. In Boston, the physician shortage is relatively less acute, although still present. There, physicians are obligated to do post-hospitalization follow-ups with those patients (lacking a regular physician) who they must take when "on call" at the hosptial. It is also easier to refer patients coming to the emergency room for general treatment to an area physician after their first visit. Physicians in the Lansing area are more likely to be too "swamped" for such referrals.

Prevalent in recent years has been the decline in G.P.'s. These men have functioned in the past to counsel, educate, and channel persons in the medical care system (see Figure 5). Lacking this guidance and personal touch, people may become confused by the myriad of specialties and not know where to turn. A well-established emergency room, where the physicians are familiar and trusted, may fill the need left by the vanishing G.P.'s.

A second reason frequently given for the increase in emergency room Medicaid patients is that many doctors are selective against Medicaid. Thus, the poor are the victims not only of the physician shortage, but also of discrimination by the few existing doctors. Common reasons given for this phenomenon were too much red tape, delay in collecting fees, and low fee rates. These same three criticisms were voiced in a national survey covering 26 states.[8]

I found one physician, however, who reasons that money is not that important in this situation. Even with less than the full regular fee, a physician can be assured of a 100 percent collection rate on Medicaid, he says. The collection rate in the emergency room runs about 75 percent, and a physician generally can expect to collect less than 100 percent. He offers three explanations: (1) A physician may resent people who are on welfare and not working, (2) the physician shortage may cause physicians to be so swamped that they can and want to be selective, or (3) some personality problems, or

Figure 5. *General Practitioners in Relation to All Physicians in Ingham County, 1963–1970*

SOURCE: Data from the American Medical Association.

NOTE: Ingham County shows a drop in *total* M.D.'s involved in patient care, while the population was climbing over the same period.

behavior which he associates with the poor may "rub a doctor the wrong way."

I conducted a telephone survey of all the general practitioners and pediatricians listed in the Lansing directory yellow pages. Two questions were posed: "Is Dr. _____ currently taking any new patients?" "Does he take Medicaid?" The results were as follows: One-half of the 34 physicians called were taking new patients; of these, 39 percent *would not* or else *preferred not* to take Medicaid patients. I gained some realization of what it means to be discriminated against on economic grounds.

On the positive side, the St. Lawrence emergency room has several features attractive to those in need of general nonemergency treatment. First, it has established a good general reputation in the community. The emergency room doctors are highly qualified, and their names are familiar in the area. Second, waiting time is usually the shortest among the top emergency rooms in the area, and there is 24-hour service, free of charge, to those covered by Medicaid.

Competing with these advantages are the area clinics. I discussed this situation at length with a hospital social worker. The Ingham

County Department of Health sponsors a number of free clinics in such areas as child health, otology, dental care, family planning, venereal disease, and prenatal care. The Lansing Model Cities program also has started a health clinic which duplicates county services in such areas as prenatal care and child health.

An important factor in the success of these clinics is the receptiveness of the communities that they serve. Too often there is a lack of communication between medical facility planners or medical personnel and the poor. As a result, expensive facilities go unaccepted and underutilized.

Other problems of the typical welfare clinic are the limited hours, the apathetic attitudes of personnel, the general impersonality of the situation, and the degrading stigma of it all. The emergency room, in contrast, is a centralized facility with a reputable physician available 24 hours a day to treat a wide range of medical problems in a relatively short time. In addition, the stigma of the clinic is not so evident, because *rich and poor sit in the same waiting room and are treated by the same doctors.*

What will happen in the future as increasing numbers of patients storm the emergency room? I received several projections from the physicians: a "new and improved" outpatient clinic, physicians' groups to handle emergency room referrals, and more physicians. I was able to discuss the first item, the clinic, in some depth with one of the physicians. He outlined definite changes for a future clinic, such as reducing the degrading waiting line, providing continuity of care, and eliminating the "sour attitude" of the personnel by staffing with persons devoted and concerned in their approach. This new-style clinic would have regular hours and be staffed largely from the nearby university. When asked if these clinics would be only for the poor, he responded that they would not be restricted, but would operate on a fee-for-service basis for those without regular physicians. This group, of course, includes a large portion of the poor. I then asked about incentives to encourage the use of the new facility instead of the emergency room. For this he proposed a referral system in which the emergency room would function as a channeling device to refer patients to the available facility(ies). This is presently done for venereal disease cases, as the county operates a free clinic for the diagnosis and treatment of venereal disease.

Variations on the clinical approach to medicine are being tried across the nation. One experiment is the Health Maintenance Organization (HMO). This is prepaid comprehensive outpatient and hospital service to persons paying an annual fee for membership. Studies show that HMOs give high quality care but have reached mainly middle income families, perhaps due to a lack of information among all groups. There have also been some complaints of a "clinical" atmosphere in the facilities. They have not succeeded in reaching the urban and rural poor.[9]

In poverty areas, one of the latest models is the Neighborhood Health Center, such as that developed in Rochester, New York. This prepaid system seeks to provide continuity in health care to each individual and minimize the impersonal clinic image. Communication with the neighborhood is enhanced by recruiting health assistants from the area to aid in "patient pursuit" — seeking out the needy and encouraging them to use the health facilities.[10]

The great defect in the clinic approach is that the poor have no alternative. Separate health delivery systems are created, one for the rich and one for the poor. The National Medical Association (NMA) views this as "segregated medicine." A past president of the NMA has stated: "The business of separate places for the poor is not in the best interest of the patient. The same doctors who treat everyone else should treat the poor."[11] One feature of the clinic is its extensive use of paramedical personnel. This means that the poor have less contact in the clinic with the physician, whereas the wealthy can afford the fees of a private physician.

Those defending the clinics argue that for the time being we must forgo equality of medical care and use efficiently what is available to meet the present crisis. The old clinic can be changed with a little money and effort, especially if the poor participate. Furthermore, while trying to reverse the effects of poverty so that the poor can "swim" in the mainstream if they choose, something must be done to improve the bad medical care at the bottom until the medical supply is expanded to meet the need.[12]

A second solution mentioned was the organization of physicians (such as pediatricians) into groups or clinics which could guarantee quick follow-up on an emergency room referral. This is being practiced in the Boston area, and I was informed that a pediatrician in Lansing is presently working on a clinic for pediatrics.

The most obvious answer to the dilemma is more physicians in order to maintain a high quality of medical care. Especially needed are family physicians who can guide the individual through the complex system and provide continuity of health care. Paramedical personnel are beneficial, but there must be an increased supply of physicians so that the poor, and not just the well-to-do, have ample access to them. This will bring the long-range goal of equality closer to reality.

One physician suggested that physicians treating the poor should be heavily subsidized by the federal government. He reasons that whenever the government wants higher productivity, such as in wheat or corn production, it simply subsidizes that area. Subsidies to those who treat the poor should heighten productivity in that area.

In conclusion, an increase in medical suppliers would enable the emergency room to make referrals with the confidence that they will receive adequate medical attention. This, in turn, will diminish emergency room traffic from ADC and other Medicaid patients, as well as those having difficulty finding a family physician. Better and faster care could then be delivered to those needing emergency treatment, and the period of waiting would diminish. The poor, as do the wealthy, would have the benefit of physicians and facilities which deliver thorough medical care with follow-up and continuity.

Notes

1. Tax Foundation, Inc., *Medicaid: State Programs after Two Years* (n.p.: 1968), p. 6.
2. Michigan Department of Social Services, *Annual Report: Fiscal 1969* (Lansing: 1969), p. 39.
3. Tax Foundation, *Medicaid*, p. 44.
4. Ibid., pp. 42–45.
5. Robert J. Haggerty, "What Type of Medical Care Can or Should Be Offered to the Urban Poor?" in *Medicine in the Ghetto,* edited by John C. Norman (New York: Meredith Corporation, 1969), pp. 253, 256.
6. Herman Miles Somers and Anne Ramsey Somers, *Medicare and the Hospitals: Issues and Prospects* (Washington, D.C.: The Brookings Institution, 1967), p. 73.
7. Haggerty, "What Type of Medical Care," p. 253.
8. Tax Foundation, *Medicaid*, p. 43.

9. Haggerty, "What Type of Medical Care," pp. 255-57.
10. "O.E.O. Centers' Contributions Still Uncertain," *American Medical News,* May 24, 1971, p. 13.
11. Ibid.
12. Alex Gerber, *The Gerber Report* (New York: David McKay Company, Inc., 1971), pp. 211, 215.

Bibliography

Gerber, Alex. *The Gerber Report.* New York: David McKay Company, Inc., 1971.

Haggerty, Robert J. "What Type of Medical Care Can or Should Be Offered to the Urban Poor?" In *Medicine in the Ghetto,* edited by John C. Norman. New York: Meredith Corporation, 1969.

"H.M.O.'s—The Key Experimental Unit in Health Plans." *American Medical News,* June 7, 1971.

Michigan Department of Social Services. *Annual Report: Fiscal 1969.* Lansing: 1969.

"O.E.O. Centers' Contributions Still Uncertain." *American Medical News,* May 24, 1971.

Somers, Herman Miles, and Anne Ramsey Somers. *Medicare and the Hospitals: Issues and Prospects.* Washington, D.C.: The Brookings Institution, 1967.

Tax Foundation, Inc. *Medicaid: State Programs After Two Years.* N.p.: 1968.

Interviews

E. C. Nakfoor, M.C.	Ingham Emergency Physicians, P.C.
J. W. Wiegenstein, M.C.	Ingham Emergency Physicians, P.C.
Gerald Wyker, M.D.	Ingham Emergency Physicians, P.C.
G. D. Clark, M.D.	Ingham Emergency Physicians, P.C.
Ms. Joanne Dexter	St. Lawrence Hospital social worker
Ms. Rose Cross	former St. Lawrence Hospital social worker
Ms. Rhinehart	Michigan Department of Social Services, income maintenance
Mr. Peterson	Michigan Department of Social Services, statistics

This paper was prepared for a course in the economics of poverty. John MacDonald was a premed student and is now a resident in internal medicine.

AN ANALYSIS OF THE DEMAND FOR ILLICIT MARIJUANA IN A UNIVERSITY COMMUNITY AND PROJECTIONS FOR THE RESULTS OF A TAX ON LEGALIZED MARIJUANA

By Christopher Mallin

These leaves make friends, and celebrate with gentle rites the vows of peace. They have given of the lonely — the friends of the imprisoned, of the exiled, of workers in mines, of fellers of forests, of sailors on the desolate seas. They are weary minds of those who build with thought and dreams the temples of the soul. They tell of hope and rest. They smooth the wrinkled brows of pain, drive fears and strange misshapen dreads from out the mind and fill the heart with rest and peace. Within their magic warp and woof some potent gracious spell imprisoned lies, that, when released by fire, doth softly steal within the fortress of the brain and bind in sleep the captured sentinels of care and grief. These leaves are the friends of the fireside, and their smoke, like incense, rises from myriads of happy homes.

— Frontispiece, *A Textbook On Tobacco*

This paper will attempt to examine the current demand for marijuana as an illegal drug with major penalties for its possession and sale. Other studies of activity in the illegal drug market have focused mainly on the operations of organized crime, which deals in addictive drugs, and have generally ignored the cannabis market. The demand analysis will be based upon empirical research done on the campus of a large midwestern university. The demand for addictive drugs is entirely different from the demand for nonaddictive cannabis, so the lack of literature in the field means that the demand analysis will be undocumented. Due to both budget constraints and political barriers to the free flow of information in the field, the analysis unfortunately must be limited to a single university community of about 40,000. Comparisons will be drawn between the demand for cannabis and that for alcoholic beverages and tobacco. The taxes on those commodities and the revenues collected therefrom will be described. Finally, projections for the revenue and regulation results of a tax on legalized cannabis will be made, on the rather shaky basis of comparing the demand for illicit grass in a small community with the results for legal alcohol and tobacco nationwide. Due to the nature of the subject matter, no specific names will be used in identifying any person or place. Any scenario described herein, however, has been taken from "real life" insofar as anyone can define reality.

The Demand for Illicit Marijuana

The consumer's object in the demand-for-marijuana game is to maximize the number of person-stoned-hours per dollar (PSH/$) spent on a retail quantity of marijuana. The PSH/$ is the most convenient measure for both the wide variation in quality and the lack of standardized measures of quantity found in the open marijuana market. Using this measure, it becomes clear why dynamite weed sells quickly for $20 an ounce, usually in half-ounce lids for $10, while poor quality cannabis sells at a more moderate rate for $10 per one-ounce lid. True dynamite will get four people stoned for three hours on a single joint, or 12 person-stoned-hours per joint. At 20 fat joints per half-ounce lid at $10 per lid, this results in 24 person-stoned-hours per dollar. Low quality weed may require four joints to get two people stoned for three hours, or 1.5 PSH per joint. At 40 joints per one-ounce lid at $10 per lid, this results in six PSH/$. That is why only freshmen buy cheap fat lids rather than small expensive lids, despite being informed about quality. By way of comparison, a large pipeful, one-fourth gram, of average hashish will get six people stoned for three hours. At $5 a gram, this yields 14.4 PSH/$. There is nothing like dynamite weed.

For consumers to maximize PSH/$, they must have a great deal of information about prices, quantities, and qualities of cannabis available in the area. This is quite difficult to obtain, since most dealers keep advertising to a minimum, and many are scared out of business if their reputation spreads too widely. The dealer's decision as to volume of sales and thus volume of information flow is based entirely on the shape of his or her risk/benefit indifference curve. To make more money, dealers must increase the volume of sales, and each additional person sold to is an additional potential informer. The dealer who adheres to the Machiavellian maxim that " 'tis better to be bold than cautious, for the Market is a woman and goes to the one who has balls" can make a fortune selling to strangers with a good information campaign, but the potentially disastrous results of that risk deter most dealers. An example is the current widening circle of arrests on this campus, stemming from the arrest several weeks ago of a high school and a university student. One or both apparently made a deal with the authorities, resulting in the arrest two weeks later of three people in the dorm from which the original two bought the dope. Over the last two weeks seven more people in the same dorm and at least two in a neighboring dorm were arrested on charges of possession and/or sale. In all of the arrests, the officers arrived with arrest warrants for specific persons rather than search warrants. The domino theory around here makes Southeast Asia look like a game.

The effect of all this is that information is hard to come by. The enforced lack of information flow leads to the potential for price discrimination within a very small geographical area. Prices are generally standardized within a single dorm supplied by two or more major dealers, but in neighboring dorms served by only a single major supplier or by casual or marginal suppliers, prices may be 25–50 percent higher. Lids sold for $10 in a large dorm with several dealers and enough intramural information flow to keep prices down have been resold by marginal dealers in adjacent dorms for $14 and in more distant dorms for $16. Clearly, the demand curve is not price-elastic within the relevant range. This sort of interdorm traffic is handled almost entirely by casual dealers, who merely pick up ten lids from a friend in the large dorm and resell them in their own dorms in order to make a quick $40, rather than by regular dealers who buy kilos and keep a steady supply on hand. A regular dealer will rarely risk interdorm sales. The consumer's problem, then, is to gain the confidence of a regular dealer; after that, his troubles are over.

The level of aggregate demand generally increases from September to June. Two phenomena are responsible for the major portion of this shift, the increase in the number of consumers and the increase in consumption per person. In September, many of the new members of the university commmunity have never tried marijuana, and most new members, both freshmen and transfers, and even newly hired faculty and staff, do not have contacts or reliable ways of making their demand known to dealers. In the first few weeks of the term, these contacts are established, and the number of consumers increases until it levels out around Thanksgiving. Between Thanksgiving and the end of the fall term, many freshmen who have kept themselves pure by abstaining from illicit drugs fall for the first time, and a large number of those become regular users. Winter term sees the largest conversion of previous nonconsumers. This is commonly attributed to the lack of anything to do comparable to football in the fall. Bored people turn to dope for the first time. By spring term, almost everyone who is going to smoke is doing so, and the number of consumers remains fairly constant from April through June, as the figure below indicates.

Per person consumption (PPC) remains stable at a relatively low level, approximately one lid a month for regular users, throughout fall term. There is a decrease in the actual amount smoked during midterms and final examinations, but these periods are usually immediately followed by excessive partying, so the variation in

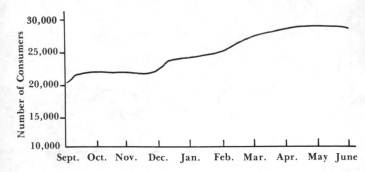

amount actually purchased is minimal. Winter term sees a large increase in per person consumption, again commonly attributed to
boredom. PPC may double to two lids a month, again with a
decrease in actual smoking toward midterms, although not so pro-
nounced as the fall term slump. By finals of winter term, spring
fever generally has struck, dependent upon the weather (a non-
economic variable quite troublesome for market research), and
there is usually no noticeable slump in aggregate consumption during that finals week. Many individuals appear to cut their consumption as during the previous term, but many more seem to increase their consumption. During spring term there is no question
of appearances. Everyone increases consumption (see the figure
below). Usage among dealers who have access to large amounts of
cheap or "free" (excluding opportunity cost) grass has been known
to rise as high as one lid a week, although among normal retail
customers consumption rarely goes above three lids a month. In
June there is often a stockpiling phenomenon, with consumers pur-
chasing one-quarter or one-half pound to last the summer.

Demand seems to be fairly inelastic over the normal range of
$10–$14 per lid, somewhat more elastic between $14 and $16, and
highly elastic above $16. Below $10, demand also becomes highly
elastic as consumers tend to stockpile at unusually low prices, as the
following figure illustrates.

There seems to be little substitution of known harmful drugs
such as amphetamines for marijuana as long as the marijuana is
available within a reasonable price range. It is usually not until
prices go above $15 a lid that consumers take to other drugs. The
most common substitute appears to be alcohol, and it has been sug-

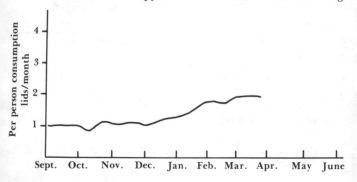

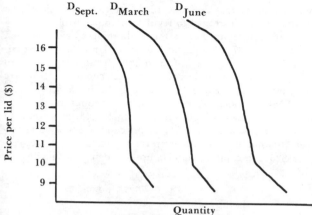

Quantity
(Write in your own scale.)

gested that party store sales in the immediate vicinity of campus are a fairly reliable index of the availability of marijuana.

The Liquor Tax

Alcoholic beverages have long been used as the base for revenue-raising taxes. The federal government has raised revenue in this manner since the Whiskey Rebellion of 1792. The federal tax on distilled spirits is currently $10.50 per gallon, which is over one-half the retail sales price of most common domestic whiskeys. State and local taxes, or state profits in monopoly states, make up at least an additional one-quarter of the retail price, generally more.[1]

The demand for alcoholic beverages seems to be quite inelastic with respect to price over a wide range. Examples of such inelasticity are beer sales at sporting events and other large gatherings, where beer that usually sells for 25 cents a can or less in a carry-out store sells for 50 cents a can. The volume of such sales is extremely high. A further example is the price of mixed drinks, which may rise 50 percent after a certain time of night in a given restaurant or lounge, without noticeable decline in volume. This is similar to the response met by marijuana profiteers who jack up prices on a campus immediately before a major concert and reap a fortune, provided they do not sell to the wrong person. The similarity in the demand curves of the two goods is a clear suggestion that as far as economic considerations are concerned, the two goods should be dealt with similarly in regard to regulation and control.

Actual public revenues from alcoholic beverages have increased from $3,020,750,637 in 1945, including $2,415,016,611 federal, $526,107,755 state, and $43,626,269 local revenues, to $7,450,999,548 in 1969, the last year for which complete figures are available, including $4,843,849,846 federal, $2,347,595,190 state, and $259,554,512 local revenues.[2] State revenues range from $4,547,342 for Alaska, which works out to $16.13 per capita, to $313,584,268 for New York, or $17.12 per capita.[3] Seven states collect over $100 million annually from the liquor tax. Six states collect over $20 per capita, New Hampshire being the highest at $24.13.[4]

The Tobacco Tax

Tobacco products have been the base for revenue-raising taxes for over a hundred years. The first tax on tobacco and cigars was imposed by Congress in 1862, the first tax on cigarettes in 1864.[5] The federal tax on cigarettes is currently eight cents a pack, for a pack costing approximately 12 cents to produce and distribute, since prior to last year's introduction of a state cigarette tax in North Carolina a pack cost 20 cents there. State taxes range from 2.5 cents in North Carolina and Virginia to 13 cents a pack in Pennsylvania.[6]

The demand for cigarettes seems to be quite inelastic with regard to price over a wide range. Per capita consumption of cigarettes in Virginia, the state with the lowest tax and hence lowest retail price, was 2,522 cigarettes in 1967, while per capita consumption in Pennsylvania, which has the highest tax and highest retail price, was 2,437 cigarettes. Consumption is probably elastic with respect to nonprice variables, as per capita consumption ranges from 1,267 in Utah to 3,742 in Nevada, and both states have an eight-cent per pack tax on cigarettes. There may be an interesting cross-elasticity waiting to be discovered between cigarette consumption and gambling, and perhaps a further correlation with the size of the stakes gambled. Per capita cigarette consumption in the District of Columbia is 4,804 annually.[7] But whatever these variables may be, they presumably do not affect the revenue results of a tax on cigarettes and are well beyond the scope of this paper.

Actual public revenues from cigarette taxes in 1967, the latest year for which figures are readily available, were $3,836,465,000, consisting of $2,111,421,000 federal revenues, $1,719,672,000 state revenues, and $5,372,000 District of Columbia revenues. State revenues ranged from $2,407,000 in Wyoming, which works out to $7.74 per capita, to $223,639,000 in New York, which amounts to $12.22 per capita. Five states collect over $100 million annually in cigarette tax revenues. Per capita revenue ranges from $3.00 in the low-tax state of Virginia to $16.27 in the moderate-tax (6.5 cents per pack) state of New Hampshire. Seventeen states collect over $10 per capita in cigarette tax revenues, all of them having a tax rate at least as high as, and mostly higher than, New Hampshire's.[8]

The Cannabis Tax

The wide inelastic range of demand for cannabis is made to order for a high-revenue excise tax. Given legalization, marijuana could be supplied as cheaply as tobacco, at less than one cent per fat joint. A 24-cent tax per joint, raising the price of a pack from its production cost of less than 20 cents to $5, the current illicit market price for half a lid of mediocre grass yielding 20 joints, would bring a lot of revenue. Virtually all the tax would be paid by the consumer, which incidence should please moralistic and/or industry-minded legislators. The possibility of a consumer rebellion in the form of home growing of dope rather than leaving the market to the cigarette companies exists, but the great urban areas of the United States would certainly consume more than they can supply for themselves. Raising the tax to excessive levels to emphasize the regulation rather than the revenue aspects of the phenomenon would certainly lead to such a consumer rebellion, and perhaps result in the continuation of the current illicit market.

Given legalization, the demand for marijuana would shift in much the same manner as the annual cyclical shift described above with regard to increase in number of consumers in the university community as more people are exposed to dope as the year progresses, except that the shift would probably take place over wide sectors of the whole society and at a much greater rate. Such a shift could conceivably cut into revenues from the liquor tax or, to a much lesser extent, even the tobacco tax. But as far as revenue alone is concerned, the increase from the cannabis tax should far outweigh any loss in the other areas. The people demand dope, and the people will be served, so the government might as well cash in on it.

Notes

1. Distilled Spirits Institute, *Public Revenues from Alcoholic Beverages 1969* (Washington, D.C.: the Institute, 1971) p. 5.
2. Ibid., p. 4.
3. Ibid., p. 11.
4. Ibid., p. 8.
5. Carl Werner, *A Textbook on Tobacco* (New York: Tobacco Leaf Publishing Co., 1914), p. 22.
6. National Tobacco Tax Association, *Comparative Cigarette Tax Collections* (Chicago: the Association, 1968), p. 8.
7. Ibid., p. 8.
8. Ibid., pp. 7-8.

This paper was written for a course in public revenues. Christopher Mallin's major was justice, morality, and constitutional law. He is an attorney and city councilman in Bedford Heights, Ohio.

POVERTY AND THE DISTRIBUTION OF INCOME AND WEALTH IN EIGHTEENTH-CENTURY SUFFOLK COUNTY

By John B. Palmer

America in the eighteenth century was, in the view of many historians, a land of tremendous opportunity. Even contemporaries marveled at the ability of the common man to better himself economically. These tremendous opportunities existed because vast amounts of cheap land were available. Any person who so desired could buy a plot of land to farm. Because this land was so cheap, wage rates were high, many men left the laboring class in order to till the earth, and the supply of laborers could not match demand.[1] Indeed, contemporaries remarked that American laborers were paid two to three times as much as those in England.[2] Colonial America thus seemed to be a paradise for the common man.

Even though this was "the best poor man's country in the world," not everyone prospered in eighteenth-century America.[3] Some could not afford to pay for their food, much less purchase land. Moreover, the much lauded "middle class" society did not extend into every locality of the thirteen colonies. It is the purpose of this study to examine one small area, Suffolk County, Massachusetts (and a few contiguous areas), to see how that society was structured and to discover the extent of poverty there.

Wealth and Income in
Eighteenth-Century Suffolk County

The body of knowledge concerning the distribution of earnings within the colony of Massachusetts is so uneven and unreliable that any efforts to generalize from the data are risky. There are no income tax records or other compilations to give even an approximation of the distribution of income. Some studies have been made, however, and the results are interesting. An idea of the relative differences in income can be obtained by comparing wage rates in Boston and nearby rural areas. Generally, in what follows all workers are characterized as unskilled; skilled artisans will be considered shortly.

It is not altogether clear that farm laborers earned any more or less than city workers. According to one study, they earned exactly the same. In 1752, for example, it is reported that both farm laborers and city workers earned 15 shillings per day, old tenor. In 1772, for both rural and urban areas, workers earned 15 shillings per day, lawful money.[4] Several interesting points may be made about these figures. First, there appeared to be no change, relatively, over time. Second, they reflect a tremendous amount of inflation. Fifteen shillings old tenor was equal to two shillings lawful money.[5] Thus, the figures represent an inflation rate of 750 percent. Since it is generally admitted that there was enormous inflation during the eighteenth century (as much as 700 percent in Boston),[6] these figures seem to have some validity. Third, the figures omit some important items. Farm workers' income in kind was not considered; these laborers usually resided with their employers and received room and board.[7] This undoubtedly would alter the figures. In addition, there was the problem of periodic unemployment. Farm workers could only work certain seasons of the year (although they resided with the farmer regardless of the season). The urban worker was a victim of periodic unemployment of a different nature. Recurring depressions (especially from nonimportation policies) played a major role in the Boston worker's inability to maintain a job.[8] The poor mariners living in Boston's North End, for example, often complained bitterly about the lack of work.[9] One might conclude that agricultural laborers earned, on balance, more than workers in Boston.

There are other problems. The figures are based on data from all the colonies and thus are probably not significant with respect to

Boston. Their only value is to give a general idea of the relative earnings of city and rural workers. Even more important, however, are the sources from which these data were extracted. A number of figures were compiled from old manuscripts, memoranda, family expense books, and similar sources, and these were used to obtain an average.[10] Their accuracy is open to serious question; it is difficult to know if there are any inherent biases. Moreover, there was no occupational breakdown. It would be helpful to know how much each category of laborer made, and that information would also serve to verify the results. However, no such data appear to be available.

It is also important to consider the differential between skilled and unskilled workers. The latter classification comprised such occupations as blacksmith, carpenter, mechanic, and tanner. It comes as no surprise that these artisans earned more than the less skilled workers, perhaps two to three times more.[11]

Another important class in eighteenth-century Suffolk County was composed of merchants and similar entrepreneurs. This small group had extensive commercial investments as well as considerable personal possessions. They clearly were the elite of Boston, and as such they earned much more than the wage earners.[12]

We can attempt to describe the income distribution of Suffolk County. There was a body of unskilled laborers, both rural and urban, who earned the least. There was a mass of skilled artisans who can probably be called "middle class." There was also a small body of merchants clearly earning more than the rest of the people. The size of the latter groups is of some interest and is reflected in the fact that a "Merchants Club" was formed in 1763 with 146 members, or 6.5 percent of the adult male population.[13] It is impossible to define the size distribution of income in more detail.

There is much more information concerning wealth as opposed to income distribution in Suffolk County. This is primarily due to the existence of probate records and tax lists which shed much light on Boston's society.

The rural areas, of course, were predominantly agricultural and thus differed greatly from Boston in land policies and distribution. Boston had at one time been a farm community, but after 1650 began developing trade and manufacturing.[14] A look at the rural areas may suggest a key to Boston's development.

There seems to be little doubt that the distribution of wealth in Suffolk County became more and more unequal throughout the eighteenth century. Of 300 inventories in 1660, 13 had estates of £900 (while three had estates over £1,500). The average estate in 1660 was worth £315. In 1765, 53 of 310 inventories had estates worth £900 (devaluated), while the top 19 averaged £2,200. The average holding was £525. These differences were not due to any increases in aggregate wealth. In 1660, 57 men had estates of less than £100, while in 1765 there were 72 (among 310 inventories). In 1660, the top four-fifths of property holders owned 7.6 times more property than the lower one-fifth; by 1765, that figure was 13.75.[15] In Waltham, Roxbury, and Milton, the top 10 percent held 46 percent of the taxable estates.[16]

While the inventories are a random sample, there are biases in these records. They indicate, however, that the distribution of wealth may have been more unequal, although not substantially. Unimproved lands were not subject to taxes and therefore were not on the lists. There is, too, a question of what kinds of personal properties were excluded, an omission which would tend to understate the inequality (although the distribution of land is a more important issue here). In addition, it seems that assessors considerably undervalued the property,[17] a fact that would also tend to understate inequality since the wealthy would have more personal property than that counted.

It seems clear that there was considerable inequality in the distribution of wealth in Suffolk County. There were some very rich men and a number of small farmers.[18] Since this inequality increased over time, it seems important that the process be investigated.

One fact that stands out in eighteenth-century Suffolk County was that land prices were rising rapidly.[19] In the town of Norton, for example, land prices increased fivefold from 1711 to 1740.[20] This is one indication that Suffolk County may not have been as democratic as some have believed. The county experienced a tremendous increase in population in the eighteenth century, but the supply of land was fixed. The population was growing at a rate of up to 5 percent annually in some towns, despite the fact that there were many settlements to the west.[21] The amount of land in Suffolk County could not be expected to support an increasing number of potential landholders. The result was a growing inequality as the lower class of farmers was forced to sell to the large landowners.

Several factors were of importance in this process. The towns were simply running out of land, which is no surprise considering the age of the settlement. In 1660, the average grant of Dedham's common lands to heads of households was 210 acres throughout a lifetime. In Watertown, Medfield, and Sudbury, the average acreage given out was 126, 150, and 150, respectively. For all of Suffolk, the average was 150. By the time of the Revolution, however, the grants were much smaller. Sudbury granted 56 acres per man, while Medfield and Waterbury averaged 44 and 38. For all of Suffolk County, the average was 43.[22] This is clear evidence that land was running out.

Another contributing factor to the growing inequality was the practice of distributing land evenly among a man's sons (with a double share for the eldest).[23] Although this would seem to have a democratizing effect, it actually contributed to the growing accumulation of land by a few. Because the farmers, on the average, had smaller parcels of land, they found it difficult to maintain a family. As early as 1721, it was noted that "many of our old towns are too full of inhabitants for husbandry."[24] Many of the farmers lived on a subsistence level.[25] Because the towns were running out of land, they were increasingly handing out marginal lands.[26] This made farming more difficult than it already was. Moreover, the farmers engaged in wasteful farming practices that reduced significantly the productivity of existing land.[27] The yield in Dedham at about midcentury was one to five bushels per acre less than in other parts of Massachusetts.[28] Poor luck and lack of business skills undoubtedly contributed to the difficulty of the small farmer.[29] The result was that those who could not subsist dropped out and migrated elsewhere, while the property was given or sold to someone else.

Boston reflected the same increasing inequality in the distribution of wealth that was prevalent in the rural areas. Measuring the taxes on personal and real estate, one historian compared the results between 1687 and 1771. In 1687, the top 15 percent had 52 percent of the taxable assets, while the top 5 percent held 25 percent. Fourteen percent of the adult males were propertyless. By 1771, the wealthiest 25 percent had 78 percent of the taxable property, while the top 5 percent had over 44 percent of all the taxable wealth. The number of propertyless males had increased to 29 percent.[30]

These results must be qualified. The lists do not include slaves or servants,[31] which presumably would increase the number of propertyless males. Moreover, there appears to be a tendency for the lists to understate the values of the rich.[32] Thus, the inequality is probably greater than that stated.

There were several reasons for the increased inequality in the distribution of wealth. First, the large increase in propertyless males was probably due to the low wages that unskilled workers received. They found it difficult to accumulate enough money to buy property,[33] in contrast to the artisans who usually owned their own houses.[34] Second, most of these propertyless workers were immigrants, either from Europe or from neighboring towns.[35] Those from England were such a burden on the town that shipowners were sometimes ordered not to bring them in.[36] Those from neighboring towns were an even more important factor, however. Some were war refugees, but by far the largest group was displaced farmers from the rural areas.[37] It has been estimated that over 70 percent of Boston's immigrants were from neighboring towns.[38] Part of the increasing inequality was due, then, to this rural to urban migration.

Another source of the growing inequality was the increasing concentration of capital in the hands of the wealthy merchants. In 1700, one-third of the adult males of Boston had interest in shipping (which was, of course, the city's main industry). By 1771, only 5 percent held shares in ships with a capacity of more than ten tons; the average ship's tonnage was roughly 112.[39] This no doubt explains why the merchants were the richest men in the colony.

Even though there was an increase in the inequality of the distribution of wealth and income, that is not sufficient reason to describe the society as undemocratic. We must also consider its mobility, both horizontal and vertical. There is no question as to horizontal mobility in Suffolk County. While there was a steady stream of migrants from the rural areas to Boston, large numbers also headed west to find a better place to make a living.[40] It was indeed a fluid society in this respect, and in many ways this was the essence of colonial American democracy.

But Boston society was also vertically mobile. For the laborer, both skilled and unskilled, there was a good chance of moving up the ladder. Of 48 artisans rated at £150 in 1780, one of four was from the ranks of the unskilled; 60 percent had more property than their fathers; 25 percent of the merchants were sons of artisans, and some were sons of mariners. Three-eighths were farmers' sons or children of European immigrants. Probably 70 percent of the merchants had risen from a lower status.[41] Fathers were reporting it increasingly difficult to control their sons' selection of occupation. Even the number of indentured servants was decreasing.[42] This is clear evidence that Boston society was fluid and mobile. There was, then, economic opportunity regardless of how unequal the distributions of income and wealth.

Poverty in Suffolk County

It is virtually impossible to estimate what percentage of the people in Suffolk County were poor. It is extremely doubtful whether even contemporaries knew. Any attempts to give a precise figure are questionable, but efforts have been made to define a "poverty line" for Suffolk County. One historian estimated that a subsistence level in the rural areas was £50, £60 in the city.[43] This calculation does not take into account the fact that many people manufactured their own products for home use.[44] Moreover, the three-person family on which it was based was rather small by eighteenth-century standards.[45] It is difficult to say how many were below the poverty line, then, although the fact that many were migrating to the city is probably evidence that they found it difficult to support families on small farms.

There are several ways to determine whether the "poor" were increasing in the eighteenth century. One is to count the number of "warnings-out" issued by the towns. According to common law, the towns were responsible for the care of the poor. For this reason, the towns had the privilege of warning out all newcomers. If the new inhabitants failed to leave, then the towns were no longer responsible for them.[46] Thus the number of such commands given indicates the public preoccupation with the problem of poverty and, indirectly, the number of poor. Evidence indicates that most of the towns increased the number of warnings-out given during the century. Dedham reported that in 1716-1717 only five people were warned out, while in 1762-1763 the number was 30. Rehoboth records report that the number of warnings-out increased sixfold between 1724 and 1757.[47] Figures are similar for other towns, but one must be suspicious of them. Some towns had a tendency to warn out extreme numbers in order to protect themselves. In the

1790s, for example, Easton warned out one-third of its population.[48] This would tend to overemphasize the problem of poverty. Yet, many ignored the warnings, and since they were not warned out each year, the figures would not include them. Even more important were the wandering poor,[49] and warnings-out probably ignored them to a large extent.

Perhaps the best way to count the number of poor is to determine who was receiving aid from the various governments. Those who could not support themselves had to be helped by someone, and it was usually the towns that provided support. It seems apparent that the number of poor in Suffolk County was increasing, although not by much. Dedham reported, for example, that from 1735 to 1764 the number of cases of poverty increased from .8 percent to 1.3 percent. The problem became so large that in 1773 a poorhouse was erected.[50] Private aid was extended, but since the greatest portion of aid to poor families was given through the government,[51] one can conclude that the number of cases indicates a small but growing problem.

It is even more difficult to determine the number of poor in Boston, but an estimate can be derived from the number of people in the almshouse. In 1742 there were 142.[52] In 1769, a special committee reported that the number of poor had been increased by the loss of trade and commerce so that 230 resided in the almshouse and 40 in the workhouse. Many were on out-relief.[53] The colony's population decreased from 16,382 in 1742 to 15,520 in 1771,[54] so these figures indicate that the number of poor increased from .9 percent to 1.7 percent from 1742 to 1769. It is not clear that this represents the whole of the problem in Boston. People considered "going on the town" a catastrophe and probably avoided doing so if at all possible. In most cases, partial relief of some sort was given,[55] but it is impossible to determine the number. One estimate is that 30-40 percent of Boston's population was poor, or "near poor," in 1790, which, interestingly enough, would probably include all the unskilled laborers. This guess was based on a "minimum subsistence level" (which was not defined) and the fact that a good number of people did not own taxable property.[56] This kind of estimation is clearly guesswork, but it does indicate that Boston was no poor man's paradise.

Who were the poor? Of those who could not help themselves, the most numerous were probably the widows of those who died fighting the Indians and French throughout the century.[57] The alms-houses included, also, a number of disabled veterans, the aged, drunkards, the insane, and illegitimate children.[58] Those who could work were put in the workhouses, although it is not clear that they actually worked. These included a large number of people generally considered "lazy" by the public and probably a number of unemployed men.[59]

It is important to note that a good portion of the poor were immigrants.[60] In 1734, for example, only 33 percent of those under local relief in Boston were native born; the rest were from outside the city or from Europe.[61] The majority came from the outlying towns. As early as 1679, this problem was recognized: "Because the Constitution of the towne of Bostone is such in respect of the continuall resort of all sorts of persons from all parts the towne is fild with poor idle and profane pesons which are greatly prejuditiall to the inhabitants."[62] It was these migrants who caused Massachusetts to break away from the tradition of locally sponsored public welfare and gradually take over the responsibility of aiding the poor.[63]

Conclusion

It has been shown that Boston and Suffolk County's social structure in the eighteenth century was not democratic. Instead, it prefigured modern industrialized society. A growing population, rising land costs, and the decreasing availability of good land forced the immigration of many of the less successful farmers to Boston, where they were members of the lower classes. This contributed to the growing inequality in Boston. It also resulted to a large extent in an increasing number of impoverished people for whom the state was forced to care.

Notes

1. Robert E. Brown, *Middle Class Democracy and the Revolution in Massachusetts* (Ithaca: Cornell University Press, 1955), pp. 1-20.
2. U.S. Bureau of Labor Statistics, *History of Wages in the United States from Colonial Times to 1928,* Bulletin No. 499 (Washington, D.C.: the Bureau, 1929), p. 7.

3. Quoted from Carl N. Degler, *Out of the Past,* in *Class and Society in Early America,* edited by Gary B. Nash (Englewood Cliffs, N.J.: Prentice-Hall, 1970), p. 18.
4. Carrol D. Wright, *Historical Review of Wages and Prices 1752–1860* (Boston: Wright and Potter, 1885), pp. 45-48.
5. Bureau of Labor Statistics, *History of Wages,* p. 17.
6. Roger W. Weiss, "The Issue of Paper Money in the American Colonies, 1720-1774," *Journal of Economic History* 30 (September 1970): 777.
7. Jackson Turner Main, *The Social Structure of Revolutionary America* (Princeton: Princeton University Press, 1965), p. 70.
8. Ibid., p. 73.
9. Allan Kulikoff, "The Progress of Inequality in Revolutionary Boston," *William and Mary Quarterly* 28 (July 1971): 388.
10. Wright, *Historical Review,* p. 45.
11. Donald R. Adams, "Some Evidence on English and American Wage Rates, 1790-1830," *Journal of Economic History* 30 (September 1970): 504; and Main, *Social Structure,* p. 75.
12. James A. Henretta, "Economic Development and Social Structure in Colonial Boston," *William and Mary Quarterly* 22 (January 1965): 87-88.
13. Ibid., p. 89.
14. Ibid., p. 75.
15. Kenneth Lockridge, "Land, Population and the Evolution of New England Society, 1630-1790," *Past and Present* 39 (April 1968): 72.
16. Main, *Social Structure,* p. 31.
17. Ibid., p. 13.
18. Ibid., p. 28.
19. Percy Wells Bidwell and John I. Falconer, *History of Agriculture in the Northern United States, 1620–1860* (New York: Peter Smith, 1941), p. 701.
20. J. M. Bumstead, "Religion, Finance, and Democracy in Massachusetts: The Town of Norton as a Case Study," *Journal of American History* 57 (March 1971): 821.
21. Nash, ed., *Class and Society,* p. 156.
22. Ibid., pp. 151-54.
23. Ibid., p. 156.
24. Ibid., p. 157.
25. Bruce Merrit, "Loyalism and Social Conflict in Revolutionary

Deerfield, Massachusetts," *Journal of American History* 57 (September 1970): 277.

26. Nash, ed., *Class and Society,* p. 155.
27. Bidwell and Falconer, *History of Agriculture,* p. 70.
28. Edward M. Cook, "Social Behavior and Changing Values in Dedham, Massachusetts, 1700 to 1775," *William and Mary Quarterly* 27 (October 1970): 571.
29. Lockridge, *Past and Present,* p. 74.
30. Nash, ed., *Class and Society,* pp. 134-42.
31. Jackson Turner Main, "Trends in Wealth Concentration before 1860," *Journal of Economic History* 31 (June 1971): 445.
32. Ibid., p. 446.
33. Main, *Social Structure,* p. 73.
34. Ibid., p. 132.
35. Kulikoff, "Progress of Inequality," p. 400.
36. Robert W. Kelso, *The History of Public Poor Relief in Massachusetts, 1680-1720* (Boston: Houghton Mifflin, 1922), p. 55.
37. Carl Bridenbaugh, *Cities in Revolt: Urban Life in America, 1743-1776* (New York: Knopf, 1955), p. 123.
38. Kulikoff, "Progress of Inequality," p. 400.
39. Nash, ed., *Class and Society,* p. 145.
40. Main, *Social Structure,* pp. 164-65.
41. Ibid., pp. 161-91.
42. Henretta, "Economic Development," p. 83.
43. Main, *Social Structure,* p. 113.
44. Rowland Berthoff, *An Unsettled People: Social Order and Disorder in American History* (New York: Harper and Row, 1971), p. 63.
45. Ibid., p. 138.
46. Josiah Henry Benton, *Warning-Out in New England* (Boston: W. B. Clarke, 1911), pp. 4-9.
47. Lockridge, *Past and Present,* pp. 72-73.
48. Kelso, *Public Poor Relief,* p. 50.
49. Ibid., p. 57.
50. Cook, "Social Behavior," p. 568.
51. Elizabeth Wisner, "The Puritan Background of the New England Poor Laws," *Social Science Review* 19 (September 1945): 381; and Robert H. Bremner, *American Philanthropy* (Chicago: University of Chicago Press, 1960), p. 24.
52. Kulikoff, "Progress of Inequality," p. 383.

53. Bridenbaugh, *Cities in Revolt,* p. 320.
54. Henretta, "Economic Development," p. 81.
55. Kelso, *Public Poor Relief,* p. 102.
56. Kulikoff, "Progress of Inequality," pp. 383-84.
57. Kelso, *Public Poor Relief,* p. 107.
58. Ibid., p. 101.
59. Marcus Wilson Jernegan, *Laboring and Dependent Classes in Colonial America, 1607-1783* (Chicago: University of Chicago Press, 1931), p. 198.
60. Bridenbaugh, *Cities in Revolt,* p. 122.
61. Jernegan, *Laboring and Dependent Classes,* p. 797.
62. *A Report of the Record Commissioners of the City of Boston,* 38 vols. (Boston: 1881), vol. 8, p. 135.
63. Kelso, *Public Poor Relief,* pp. 101-23.

Bibliography

Adams, Donald R., Jr. "Some Evidence on English and American Wage Rates, 1790-1830." *Journal of Economic History* 30 (September 1970): 499-520.

Benton, Josiah Henry. *Warning-Out in New England.* Boston: W. B. Clarke Co., 1911.

Berthoff, Rowland. *An Unsettled People: Social Order and Disorder in American History.* New York: Harper and Row, 1971.

Bidwell, Percy Wells, and John I. Falconer. *History of Agriculture in the Northern United States, 1620-1860.* New York: Peter Smith, 1941.

Bremner, Robert H. *American Philanthropy.* Chicago: University of Chicago Press, 1960.

Bridenbaugh, Carl. *Cities in Revolt: Urban Life in America, 1743-1776.* New York: Alfred A. Knopf, 1955.

Brown, Robert E. *Middle Class Democracy and the Revolution in Massachusetts, 1691-1780.* New York: Cornell University Press, 1955.

Bumstead, J. M. "Religion, Finance, and Democracy in Massachusetts: The Town of Norton as a Case Study." *Journal of American History* 57 (March 1971): 817-83.

Cook, Edward M., Jr. "Social Behavior and Changing Values in Dedham, Massachusetts, 1700 to 1775." *William and Mary Quarterly* 27 (October 1970): 546-80.

Handlin, Oscar, and Mary Klug Handlin. *Commonwealth: A Study of the Role of Government in the American Economy, Massachusetts, 1774–1861*. Rev. ed. Cambridge, Mass.: Belknap Press, 1969.

Hart, Albert Bushnell, ed. *Commonwealth History of Massachusetts*. 5 vols. New York: Russell and Russell, 1966. Volume 2.

Henretta, James. "Economic Development and Social Structure in Colonial Boston." *William and Mary Quarterly* 22 (January 1965): 75–92.

Jernegan, Marcus Wilson. *The American Colonies: 1492–1750*. New York: Frederick Ungar Publishing Co., 1929.

— — —. *Laboring and Dependent Classes in Colonial America: 1607–1783*. Chicago: University of Chicago Press, 1931.

Kelso, Robert W. *The History of Public Poor Relief in Massachusetts, 1620–1920*. Boston: Houghton Mifflin Co., 1922.

Kulikoff, Allan. "The Progress of Inequality in Revolutionary Boston." *William and Mary Quarterly* 27 (July 1971): 375–412.

Lockridge, Kenneth. "Land, Population and the Evolution of New England Society, 1630–1790." *Past and Present* 39 (April 1968): 62–80.

— — —. "The Population of Dedham, Massachusetts, 1636–1736." *Economic History Review* 19 (August 1966): 318–44.

Main, Jackson Turner. *The Social Structure of Revolutionary America*. Princeton, N. J.: Princeton University Press, 1965.

— — —. "Trends in Wealth Concentration before 1860." *Journal of Economic History* 31 (June 1971): 445–50.

Merrit, Bruce G. "Loyalism and Social Conflict in Revolutionary Deerfield, Massachusetts." *Journal of American History* 57 (September 1970): 277–89.

Nash, Gary B., ed. *Class and Society in Early America*. Englewood Cliffs, N. J.: Prentice-Hall, Inc., 1970.

Report of the Record Commissioners of the City of Boston, 38 vols. Boston: Rockwell and Churchill, 1881.

U.S. Bureau of Labor Statistics. *History of Wages in the United States from Colonial Times to 1928*. Bulletin No. 499. Washington, D.C.: U.S. Government Printing Office, 1929.

Weeden, William B. *Economic and Social History of New England, 1620–1789*. 2 vols. Boston: Houghton Mifflin Co., 1891. Volume 2.

Weiss, Roger W. "The Issue of Paper Money in the American Colonies, 1720-1774." *Journal of Economic History* 30 (September 1970): 770-84.

Wisner, Elizabeth. "The Puritan Background of the New England Poor Laws." *Social Science Review* 19 (September 1945): 381-90.

Wright, Carroll D. *Historical Review of Wages and Prices.* Boston: Wright and Potter, 1885.

This paper was written for a course entitled The Economics of Poverty. John Palmer majored in history and is now a tax attorney with a firm in Chicago.

A STUDY OF THE RELATIONSHIP BETWEEN EXTERNAL DISECONOMIES AND POPULATION

By Christine Schneider Schafer
and
Daniel Watson

In his text, *Urban Economics,* [1] Harry W. Richardson formulates an hypothesis about the effects of external economies and diseconomies which he says is relevant not only to the study of location theory, but also to the entire field of urban economics. General conclusions, which can be derived from considering agglomeration economies and their related external economies, are relevant to such areas as growth, transport, urban renewal, fiscal problems, and planning as well as location theory. The hypothesis that Richardson proposes, based on work of W. J. Baumol, is that cities have already reached or exceeded their optimal size because external diseconomies are increasing faster than population. [2]

It is easy enough to give a long list of agglomeration and external economies. The problem arises when we attempt to quantify their impact. It is probable that the character of urban growth and the size distribution of urban centers are determined largely by the balance of external economies and diseconomies. [3]

The problem is our lack of understanding whether urban concentration confers net social costs or benefits, or, if the answer to this depends on the size of the concentrations, where the optimal point occurs.

The function Baumol outlined for the relationship between external diseconomies and population can be stated as: $D = AP^2$, where D is the external diseconomy, and P is the population. What is implied in this relationship is that external diseconomies or social costs which people incur in ordinary living, but do not pay for, rise considerably faster than the population. In fact, they go up with the square of the population. From this functional relationship, Baumol was able to conclude that the larger the city, the greater the per capita costs involved in maintaining that city. This has important implications in modern society as urban sprawl becomes an increasingly more familiar phenomenon. Baumol concludes that city size should be kept at a minimum to minimize the costs of the external diseconomies.

The reasoning behind this assumption is clear. If each inhabitant in an area imposes external costs on every other, and if the size of the costs borne by each individual is about proportional to the population, then (since these costs apply to each of the n persons involved) the total external costs will vary not in proportion to n but to n^2.[4]

An important question arises. Richardson takes issue with the statement that the exponent is always an even two. It is questionable whether each individual imposes his or her total costs on every other individual (thereby multiplying the costs to the square of the population) or whether some of the costs are shared among the residents so that the exponent is something less than two. Richardson makes the case that the exponent will be less than two, although still greater than one. He goes on to say that it will vary with population size. This variance is needed, he says, to account for the transition from net economies to net diseconomies, something Baumol failed to consider. Although this variance is an important consideration, it is most important to know just what that exponent is for external diseconomies and how rapidly those costs go up in relation to population. With that information in hand, a study could be made to determine the relationship of external economies to population. By putting these two relationships together, the point could be found at which they cross, and optimal city size could be determined.

This paper will attempt to ascertain the relationship between external diseconomies and population, or what the exponent in the function actually is.

To begin, we chose some external costs common to cities of all sizes and randomly selected cities with populations of varying sizes. Then the relationship between the size of the cities and these costs could be established. We selected for observation the varying cost of urban services in cities of different sizes. This was a variable proposed by Richardson and seemed to be a measure highly representative of external costs and easily measurable in relation to city size.

Data were gathered by interviewing the city clerk of each city chosen to determine the annual fiscal budget for 1971–1972. By recording actual expenditures (as opposed to appropriations) for each of the services provided by the city government, it was possible to compile a list of ten services which were common to each city. These were recorded in a like manner so that the numbers being compared measured similar services. After directly interviewing 15 city clerks and obtaining about ten usable budgets, it was learned that an organization called the Michigan Municipal League in Ann Arbor kept a file of copies of fiscal budgets from a number of Michigan cities. By using the copies of budgets located there and the ten already collected, we were able to compile a list of 28 cities ranging in population from 2,000 to 1.5 million, each with ten common services: police, fire, highways, sewerage, sanitation, parks and recreation, water utility, financial administration, judicial costs, and election costs. This represents a range of costs associated with a range of population.

Several constraints are inherent in this kind of study and the use of these particular factors. We tried to keep all other possible influences constant so as to have a result which directly relates only costs to the way they are affected by population increases. A primary question is, of course, whether a study of the costs of urban services is a study of externalities or merely of the demand for those services. It might be argued that the cost of urban services is not affected by externalities, but by the demand in a particular community for those services. It is possible that Detroit citizens want more police per person because they like the idea of a larger per capita police force more than do citizens in a smaller town. But here we are making an assumption. It can be assumed that city government tries to economize as much as possible and that the necessary quality of service is approximately the same per person no matter what the size of the city. By taking a large sample with a diversity of urban services, it can be assumed that per capita demand will remain fairly constant and that any increase in total demand will be a result of the greater number of persons in a confined area. In addition, it is possible that the makeup of the city in terms of income, race, and types and quantities of businesses and manufacturing causes the cost differences.

We have tried to keep any error due to this kind of variation to a minimum by randomly selecting cities and including several different cities of similar size. Although this element will cause considerable variation, on the average the function derived should approximate very closely the actual relationship. The purpose in selecting a large number of urban services as variables, each unrelated to the other, was to ensure variation within the function. As a final constraint, it is possible that location has a determining effect on the cost of urban services. To minimize this variable, the cities were selected randomly, with no relation between location and size.

On the whole, although there are several factors which cause considerable variation in the function, the constraints have been minimized, and the results obtained should give a reasonably accurate picture of the relationship between external costs and population.

After gathering our data, we wished to determine two things from it. First, we assumed that the costs of a city increase when the population rises to some exponential degree. One of our objectives was to ascertain the nature of this relationship or the size of the exponent. Second, we wished to measure the degree of association between the independent variables (size of the city population) and dependent variables (such city costs as police and fire protection). To accomplish these two objectives, regression analysis was employed to determine the nature of the relationship, and correlation analysis was used to measure the strength of the association of the two.

Regression analysis serves two purposes. First, we are able to calculate estimated values for our dependent variable for any independent variable we wish to use. This is accomplished through a regression line which depicts the relationship between x (our independent variable) and E (our dependent variable) by providing average values for E given an x. Second, regression analysis is used to obtain a measure of the error resulting from estimation of these average E values. This is accomplished through calculation of the standard error of the estimate ($S_{E.x}$), which measures the dispersion of the observed E variables around the regression line. This estimated error allows us to estimate the strength of the relation between the two variables.

In our analysis we used the independent variable X to represent various size populations taken from 28 cities and the dependent variable E, of which there are as many as ten for each of the cities. The dependent variable represents some of the costs of maintaining a city. The analysis includes costs for police, fire, highways, sewerage, sanitation, parks and recreation, water utility, financial administration, judicial costs, and election costs.

The first step was to determine the appropriate regression equation, $E = a + bX$, where b = the slope of the line and a = the E intercept. Since we are trying to find the exponent value for our population, we transformed our original equation by taking the log values of the variables. Therefore, in the equation and throughout the analysis, the variables are in fact the log of population ($\log P = X$) and the log of the costs ($\log D = E$). The reason for taking logs can be seen by referring to the original equation, $D = AP^2$. Taking the log of both sides of the equation produces $\log D = \log A + 2 \log P$, which in the notation of our regression line is $E = a + 2X$. However, we are trying to test whether the exponent is two or some other number. When we estimate our regression line, $E = a + bX$, the slope or coefficient of X will be an estimate of the exponent, and that is what we were trying to determine.

We can find a and b through a shortcut method after first calculating some of the following values:

$\overline{E} = \Sigma E/n$, where n = size of the sample; and
$\overline{X} = \Sigma X/n$.

The method of least squares was used to obtain the best fit to the regression line. This line is characterized by minimizing the sum of the squared deviations $[\Sigma(E - E)^2]$ and balancing the sum of the absolute deviations so that they equal zero. From this method, a and b are found, so that $a = \overline{E} - b\overline{X}$, and $b = \Sigma XE - n\overline{X}\ \overline{E}/\Sigma X^2 - n\overline{X}^2$.

From these variables, the regression line can be found. We first choose a population size (X) for which we wish to ascertain the city expenditures on various services. This is done by substituting our determined a and b values and predetermined X values in the formula

$$E = a + bX,$$

and our *estimated* E value is thus determined.

Now that we have determined our regression line, we show a, b, E, and X for all ten costs. The amount of error from using this line is measured. The accuracy of the line is a function of the amount of dispersion and is termed the "standard error of the estimate." It is measured by the following formula:

$$S_{E.X} = \sqrt{\frac{\Sigma(E - \bar{E})^2}{n}} ,$$

where $S_{E.X}$ is the standard error of the estimate of the dependent variable E given the independent variable X. This formula is then squared to give us the variance of E given X, which is used in estimating the strength of association between the actual and predicted values of E.

After making these calculations, we can then determine the slope of each regression line, which is our value of b. Because we have transformed our equation into logarithms, this b value also represents the exponent, since $E = aP^b$ as previously shown and b is a number hypothesized to be greater than one but less than two.

The important statistics derived from the regression analysis (and subsequently recalculated using a standard computer program for calculating regressions) are displayed in Table 1. The estimate of the coefficient of population is less than one in only two of the ten cases, and it is less than two in all cases. Using an estimate of the standard error of the coefficient of population and realizing that this coefficient is known to conform to Student's t distribution, we can establish 90 percent confidence intervals for the exponents. As we can see, there is 90 percent certainty that in six of the cases the exponent lies between one and two. In no case does two itself lie within the 90 percent confidence interval.

After determining our population exponent, we proceeded to determine the strength of the relation. The assumptions made are that (1) both X and E are random variables, (2) they are normally distributed, (3) conditional probability distributions are normal

Table 1. *Log Linear Regressions of Various Expenditures on Population*

					Dependent variable (log of)					
	Police	Fire	Highways	Sewerage	Sanitation	Parks and recreation	Water utility	Financial adminis-tration	Judicial costs	Election costs
Estimated log of constant term (lnA)	.17	-.41	1.32	.08	.83	.14	.80	2.38	-.63	-1.64
Estimated coefficient of log of population (b)	1.25	1.33	.92	1.17	1.01	1.14	1.05	.64	1.20	1.23
Standard error of population coefficient (b)	.070	.063	.085	.00	.069	.084	.156	.087	.068	.128
90 percent confidence interval for population coefficient (b)	1.16-1.34	1.25-1.41	.81-1.04	1.04-1.30	.92-1.10	1.03-1.25	.85-1.25	.53-.75	1.11-1.29	1.06-1.40
Coefficient of determination for the equation (r²)	.92	.94	.86	.87	.90	.88	.66	.73	.94	.86
Number of cities with data available	28	28	20	23	25	28	25	22	20	17
Standard error of estimate	.24	.21	.25	.28	.23	.29	.51	.21	.19	.33

with the same standard deviation for X, and (4) the preceding holds true for E.

The relationship is determined through the use of the variance of $\bar{E}$ and the variance around the regression line. The coefficient of determination, r^2, is calculated from the following formula:

$$r^2 = 1 - S_{E \cdot X}^2 / S_E^2,$$

where S_E^2 represents the total deviation, and $S_{E \cdot X}^2$ is the variance unexplained by the regression line. When subtracted from one, the fraction left (or r^2) represents the percentage of the variance in E explained by the regression equation. The r^2 value ranges from zero to one, and the closer it is to one, the higher the correlation. In contrast, the closer it is to zero, the lower the correlation. As can be seen from Table 1, we established that a strong degree of correlation exists. In other words, 92 percent of the variance in police costs, for example, is explained by the regression.

The results of our study indicate that the population exponent with which we were concerned is, generally, greater than one and less than two. We were also able to show that there is a *very* strong relationship between costs and population (shown by the exceedingly large r^2 values). What this means in terms of today's cities is that, as Baumol hypothesized, external diseconomies rise faster than the population. In other words, the closer the city population is to zero, the lower the external costs and per capita expense of maintaining the city, and thus the more efficient (in one sense) the city is.

Baumol tried to conclude from this kind of study that cities have already exceeded their optimal size and that the smaller the cities, the better. However, in light of Richardson's assertion that this relationship holds not only for diseconomies but also for economies, it would be a hazardous assumption to conclude that these Michigan cities are already too large.

Nevertheless, a useful tool is to be found here. Theoretically, if this kind of study could be combined with a study in economies of urban size, the functions could be overlapped to determine their point of intersection. At that point it would not be economical for cities to increase in size, and any addition to population beyond that point would add more to the diseconomies than to the economies. That point might lie somewhere in the future with a city much larger than any we have today, but we cannot exclude the very real possibility that modern cities are already more diseconomical than economical. We do know that costs rise faster than population and that unless benefits increase as rapidly, cities should remain small.

Notes

1. Harry W. Richardson, *Urban Economics* (Middlesex, Eng.: Penguin Books Ltd., 1971).
2. Richardson adds another dimension to the question which nullifies Baumol's assumption that he can determine optimal city size with his relationship as it applies, in addition, to external economies. This says that external economies also go up faster than population so that a study would have to be done to determine which outweighs the other, economies or diseconomies, before an optimal city size could be determined. A point such that the marginal diseconomies equal the marginal economies would be the optimum size for a city.
3. Richardson, *Urban Economics*, p. 17.
4. Richardson, *Urban Economics*, p. 18.

This paper was written for a course in urban economics. The authors wish to acknowledge that Daniel Saks helped with revisions and used the computer to calculate some statistics. Christine Schneider Schafer majored in business administration. She is an attorney with a Detroit firm. Daniel Watson, an economics major, received the J.D. degree from Wayne State University and is now an attorney.

THE INCREASED PRICE TO STUDENTS OF LIVING CLOSER TO THE UNIVERSITY

By Craig Weaver

The location decisions of people and businesses and the prices related to different locations have long been studied by urban economists. Much research has been done regarding the location decisions of businesses in urban areas. Similarly, the decision process of people in choosing housing has been well studied, especially that of low income people. Research has produced a number of well-developed theories and models, such as the concentric zones model, bid-rent and ceiling rent analysis, and the radial sectors model, to explain the behavior of these various segments of society.

One segment, however, has received relatively little study: the large number of students at our nation's colleges and universities. Anyone who has lived in or visited a college town has certainly noticed many similarities between the student market for housing and that of the low income inner city resident, especially the high density of housing and the high rents. As stated earlier, bid-rent analysis may explain the characteristics of the inner city housing market. The student housing market appears to be an ideal area in which to test this theory.

Specifically, I intend to examine the pricing of housing in student areas, primarily in East Lansing, Michigan. It is my contention that the price of housing in East Lansing is related to the distance of that housing from the Michigan State University campus. In other words, as the distance from campus decreases, the price of housing similar to that farther away will increase.

Theory

This contention is based on bid-rent analysis and utility theory. Bid-rent analysis is usually discussed in connection with business location decisions. It states that a business will choose and pay rent for a location when the marginal costs of that location equal the marginal revenue. Consequently, a downward sloping bid-rent curve can be drawn connecting the points for each distance from some central place at which marginal costs will equal marginal revenue. Finally, if the rent a business will pay for a location is the highest any business will pay for that location, then the actual price paid will coincide with the business's bid-rent curve. The primary assumption in this theory is that a large value is put on accessibility to a central point and that this value is composed mainly of transportation and time costs.

In discussing the location decisions of students, we can adapt this theory to say that a student will pay a price for a location such that his marginal costs will equal his marginal benefits; we assume utility maximization on the part of the student rather than profit maximization. As a student moves to a location nearer campus, his marginal benefits will be the increase in accessibility; his marginal costs will be the change in rent. Thus, for the student's marginal benefits to equal marginal costs, the change in rent must be exactly equal to the student's value of increased accessibility to campus.

To determine what the marginal benefits will be, we can turn to utility theory. This tells us that for any two factors a curve can be constructed which represents combinations of the two factors of equal utility to a person (see Figure 1). From this indifference curve we can construct a demand curve for accessibility. If a person's budget is held constant and the price of accessibility is allowed to change, with the use of isocost lines we can determine the optimal level of accessibility to the person for each price (Figure 2). This, then, gives us the demand curve for accessibility, shown in Figure 3.

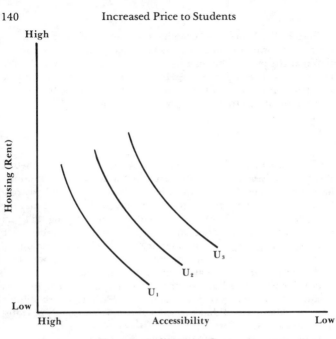

Figure 1. *Indifference Curves*

From Figure 3 it is apparent that the demand curve for accessibility will be downward sloping, assuming the other diagrams are correct, that is, that students will be willing to pay a higher price for housing nearer the campus. The limit of that price will be the point at which the additional cost of that housing as opposed to housing farther from campus will equal the additional benefits of being closer to campus. Assuming that students are the highest bidders for housing around the campus, it would follow that the price of housing in the area will vary in a manner similar to the bid-rent curve shown in Figure 4.

Design

In order to test this hypothesis empirically, a simple design was used. Specifically, 123 apartments in the East Lansing area were surveyed as to their rent and the distance of each from the Michigan State University campus. The data were then graphed to deter-

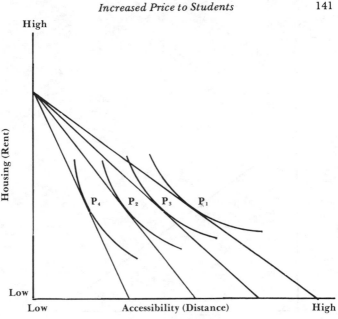

Figure 2. *Optimal Levels of Accessibility*

mine if apartments in the area did, indeed, show the expected relationship between rents and distance. Several points about this
survey require further comment.

Rent

Because apartments differ in quality, an attempt had to be made
to adjust the rent data for these differences in order to allow comparison among apartments. Several adjustments were made. First,
apartments were divided into four categories: one-bedroom furnished, two-bedroom furnished, one-bedroom unfurnished, and
two-bedroom unfurnished (with comparisons to be made only
within each category). Second, many apartments charge two rents
based on the length of the rental contract (nine or twelve months);
in all cases the price used was based on a twelve-month contract,
although this may have the effect of understating the price students
are paying, since whenever two prices are offered they usually opt

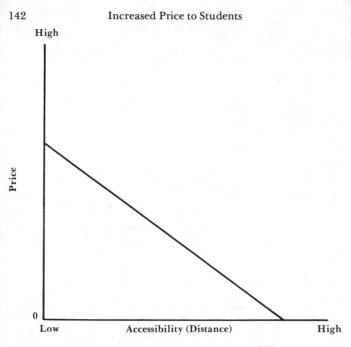

Figure 3. *Demand Curve for Accessibility*

for the higher priced, nine-month contract. Finally, no adjustment was made for such extras as swimming pools, two bathrooms, or dishwashers. In most cases the portion of the rent attributable to these factors was difficult to determine, and when estimation was possible, they proved to be relatively insignificant.

Distance

The distance used was the straight-line distance from the apartment to a single point on campus. One possibility would have been to measure the distance to the closest border of campus, but a single point, Bessey Hall, was chosen for the following reason. Most students travel to campus for the purpose of attending classes, hence transportation and time costs differ at different points within the campus border. For example, Cedar Village and Marigold apartments are both equidistant from different segments of the

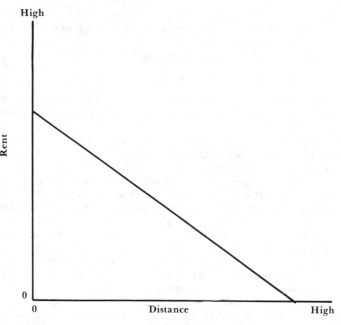

Figure 4. *Bid-Rent Curve*

campus border, yet tenants of Cedar Village perceive themselves as much closer to campus than do Marigold tenants. For this reason, a point had to be chosen which closely coincided with the point students unconsciously use to measure accessibility. Bessey Hall was chosen because it was at the center of an area with a high density of classrooms and students.

Second, apartments were aggregated into seven distance classifications: zero to one-half mile, one-half to one, one to one and one-half, one and one-half to two, two to three, three to four, and four miles and beyond. These will be referred to as groups 1, 2, 3, 4, 5, 6, and 7, respectively.

Data

Among the 123 apartments surveyed, usable data were obtained from 95; the others were rejected for various reasons, such as a small student population. Of the 95 apartments, rents were calculated for each category by finding the mean rent of the relevant apartments, shown in Table 1.

The graphs of these data appear as shown in Figure 5.

Results

Do the data support the hypothesis that rent will decrease with increasing distance from campus? The graphs in Figure 5 do indeed show this to be true.

The results for furnished apartments (a heavy student concentration) show the greatest decline in rents with distance. There were no furnished apartments between two and four miles from campus, and only a few two-bedroom furnished apartments beyond four miles. Within this two-mile radius from campus, however, the rent for two-bedroom furnished apartments was 30 percent lower for group 4 apartments than for group 1 apartments, while one-bedroom apartments were 17 percent less expensive in group 4 than in group 1. Moreover, the rents for both one- and two-bedroom furnished apartments decreased with distance at an increasing rate. The decline for two-bedroom units was 5 percent between group 1 and group 2, 10 percent between groups 2 and 3, and 15 percent between groups 3 and 4. Similarly, rents declined 2 percent for one-bedroom units between groups 1 and 2, 5 percent between 2 and 3, and 10 percent between 3 and 4. These data are shown in Figure 6.

The data for unfurnished apartments show a similar, although not as marked, decline in rents. In this case, there were no apartments in group 1, zero to one-half mile from campus. Between

Table 1. *Distance and Mean Rent Calculations*

Distance	Unfurnished		Furnished	
	1 Bed	*2 Bed*	*1 Bed*	*2 Bed*
0–1/2 mile	a	a	$214	$320
1/2–1 mile	$190	$210	$206	$305
1–1-1/2 miles	$182	$208	$197	$274
1-1/2–2 miles	$174	$202	$175	$233
2–3 miles	$180	$207	a	a
3–4 miles	$171	$199	a	a
4 or more miles	$166	$184	a	$210

[a]No or insufficient data.

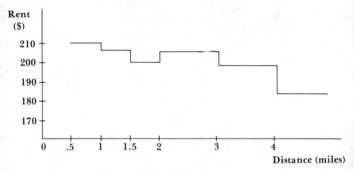

Figure 5A. *Two Bedroom, Unfurnished*

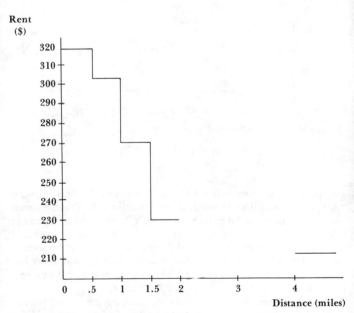

Figure 5B. *Two Bedroom, Furnished*

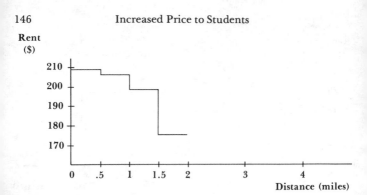

Figure 5C. *One Bedroom, Furnished*

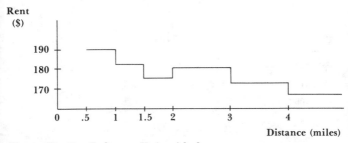

Figure 5D. *One Bedroom, Unfurnished*

groups 2 and 6, there was a 13 percent decrease in rents for both one- and two-bedroom unfurnished apartments. One-bedroom apartments decreased 4 percent between groups 2 and 3, 4 percent between 3 and 4, increased 3 percent between 4 and 5, decreased 4.5 percent between 5 and 6, and decreased 3.5 percent between 6 and 7. Similarly, for these same groups two-bedroom units decreased one percent, decreased 3 percent, increased 2.4 percent, decreased 4 percent, and decreased 7 percent.

Several comments must be made concerning the results for the unfurnished apartments. First, an increase in rents occurred for

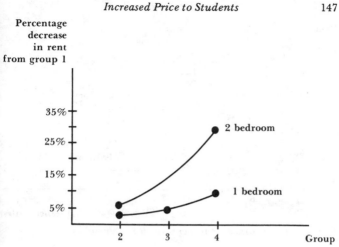

Figure 6. *Furnished Apartments*

apartments between two and three miles from campus, which is inconsistent with the trend of the results. Included in this group, however, are numerous "luxury" apartments with many extras, such as health clubs and club houses, and the student population in them is sparse. If these apartments are excluded from the data, as they probably should be, the average rent in this group of the student-occupied apartments is $175 for two-bedroom units and $150 for one-bedroom units, or a 13 percent and 12 percent decrease, respectively, from the next group closer to campus.

A closely related question is why unfurnished apartments show a smaller decrease in rent. Again, this is surely related to the percentage of students in these apartments. It was found that students tend to rent furnished more often than unfurnished apartments; hence the data for furnished apartments are more likely to reflect the most accurate distance-rent relationship for students since these are almost completely populated by students. Because unfurnished apartments have a lower student population, the distance-rent relationship for these student tenants would certainly be distorted because most of the tenants, who are nonstudents, have different bid-rent curves for apartment housing. In fact, it was found that unfurnished apartments beyond three miles had a very small stu-

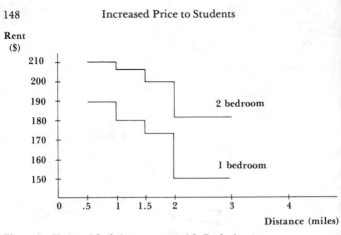

Figure 7. *Unfurnished Apartments (with Exclusions)*

dent population. If the data from these units are excluded, along with the nonstudent "luxury" apartments discussed earlier, the graph of the relationship of rents to distance appears as in Figure 7, which is much more consistent with the findings for furnished apartments.

Conclusion

The results of this study strongly support the hypothesis that the price of housing in East Lansing is inversely related to the distance of that housing from the Michigan State University campus. Admittedly, the method used to test this hypothesis was rather simple and open to error. Many variables undoubtedly were ignored, the most important being those related to costs. In this study, all differences in rents were assumed to be due to accessibility, yet other factors are important, such as varying building and capital costs. There are also probably errors involved in measuring distance by a straight line rather than by the distance students must travel.

Even accepting a possible degree of error in the results, the large differences in rents found in East Lansing are so substantial as to show that a definite relationship exists between rents and distance. Indeed, it appears that students place an extremely high value on accessibility to the campus and are willing to pay for this accessibility in the form of higher rents.

This paper was prepared for a course in urban economics. Craig Weaver was working on a master's degree in the School of Labor and Industrial Relations when this paper was written. He is currently an employee relations representative for a large firm.